AROUND THE WORLD IN GAA DAYS

Aaron Dunne currently lives in Australia, but was brought up in Ireland. He is the deputy editor of the *Irish Echo* in Sydney and formerly worked as the sports editor for the Gazette Group of Newspapers in Dublin.

AROUND THE WORLD IN
GAA DAYS

AARON DUNNE

MAINSTREAM
PUBLISHING

EDINBURGH AND LONDON

In memory of Denis Byrne, and dedicated to
the hard-working people of the GAA around the world

First published in Great Britain in 2009 by
MAINSTREAM PUBLISHING COMPANY
(EDINBURGH) LTD
7 Albany Street
Edinburgh EH1 3UG

ISBN 9781845963637

A catalogue record for this book is available
from the British Library

Typeset in Caslon and Franklin Gothic

Printed in Great Britain by
CPI Mackays of Chatham Ltd, Chatham, ME5 8TD

CONTENTS

FOREWORD

More than once, but less than a dozen times, it has been my pleasure to 'parachute' into distant foreign cities and land safely and securely within a GAA club. Always the welcome is genuine and warm, though I've never had the experience of flying east from Dublin airport. It has always been west. Always the United States and Canada, where I quickly find myself amongst new friends in New York, Toronto, Chicago or San Francisco. On some occasions, I have been asked to make a fleeting, literally flying, visit and often it seems my feet barely hit the ground.

One Saturday morning I flew out from Dublin for New York. That evening I ate in a local steakhouse and had a couple of beers, then the following afternoon met my new teammates from the Armagh GAA club, talked through our game plan for the New York junior football championship semi-final, watched Kerry's ageing legend Mick O'Connell make a cameo appearance for our opponents in Gaelic Park with ten minutes left in the game, showered at speed, then hightailed it back to JFK for a Sunday evening flight home.

Normally, however, I get to enjoy some time with my 'new club'.

Once I spent three wonderful weeks with the fantastic and lovable men and women of the Wolfe Tones club in Chicago. They shared their lives and their homes with me. They also shared their twin loves for their adopted home, and for their parishes and counties of origin.

AROUND THE WORLD IN GAA DAYS

What is always most apparent to me on all these visits is just how 'secure' everyone feels about being Irish – and about being GAA folk – in such far-flung and very different places in the world. Playing Gaelic football and hurling was, to my hosts, the most natural thing in the whole wide world. It didn't matter whether the field was too small or too wide, or whether (as was the case for the Chicago senior football championship final in 1983) the field had been borrowed from a local city high school and had American football posts at either end.

In this book, Aaron Dunne has indeed embarked on a 'true' GAA adventure. This has to be the case when someone leaves Dublin airport and heads east. The people and sights and cities that Aaron encounters are vastly different to any that I, or any other 'mercenaries' from the Meath football team of 1980–92, would ever have experienced. But throughout the journey with him in search of our games there is a recurring theme – that the Gaelic Athletic Association can make the earth a very small, familiar, happy place.

To all of those who we meet in this unique book, and who are secure and happy in their GAA lives in such distant spots on the planet, I wish you well. We, too, would love to visit you one day. Kick a ball. Sit down on the sideline. Share a drink when the sun goes down, agreeing what a great little country we come from, and what two great little games we own.

Liam Hayes
Meath footballer 1980–92
Meath footballer and parachutist 1983–86

INTRODUCTION

THE JOURNEY IS BORN

SUNDAY, 24 JUNE 2007 – CROKE PARK

It's late June, and Croke Park is rocking to the sound of the Dubs in full flow. They've been unstoppable in Leinster now for the last few years and Offaly are the latest early summer victims in another pretty pointless provincial romp. There's about ten minutes left, but the game is long over. The songs are belting out of Hill 16, but I'm struggling to stay awake. Only the soothing tones of Mícheál Ó Muircheartaigh on RTÉ Radio 1 are keeping me conscious.

Dublin have just kicked a meaningless wide, but Mícheál has somehow managed to keep the listener's ear trained on his every word. The latest stoppage has given him the opportunity to digress somewhat from the match in hand. He tends to do that, you know. This is something he's clearly been waiting quite a while to address, though. You can sense the excitement in his voice as he relays the news that surely no one was expecting to hear. The Singapore Gaelic Lions have just won the Senior Football Championship of Asia.

Taken somewhat aback, I look around at the heads beside me in the Hogan Stand. I'm eager to see if anyone else has heard it, too, or whether I had just nodded off and dreamt the whole thing. I notice an elderly gentleman, about three seats up, who has a little wireless radio with him. He must have heard. He cracks a little smile in my direction and shrugs his shoulders, seeming happy enough to laugh it off and move on. I, on the other hand, am completely fascinated. The international GAA bug just dug in its fangs.

Who the hell are the Singapore Gaelic Lions? And what are these Asian championships when they're at home? I consult Google the second I get home and the more I investigate the situation, the more I am stunned at just how many GAA clubs there are outside our little island. Sure, everybody's heard about the history in London, the traditions in New York and Boston, even the new teams popping up in Paris and Luxembourg. But Japan? Vietnam? Fiji? Turns out there are more than 200 GAA clubs outside Europe alone. I was blown away.

My mind had been wandering towards a year Down Under or a few months in Asia at the time. Anything to allay the increasingly punishing realisation that I might spend the rest of my life without ever seeing a rainless summer or living in a city with decent public transport. It poured down for the next 40 days through July and August. Decision made. I would take a year out to meet, train and play with as many international GAA clubs as was humanly possible. Time to pack a bag.

Although a lifelong GAA man, I'd never been much of a footballer or hurler myself. A long, and ultimately fruitless, underage career in Gaelic games (not including that one glorious under-16 'A' Dublin hurling league medal) had made sure I was fully versed in the limits of my own onfield abilities. All the same, my love for GAA had never waned.

The thoughts of Croker in the summer as the Dubs rolled into action or Semple Stadium in late spring as the Munster hurling championship took off were porridge to my soul each year. And no doubt they always will be. This may sound a little odd, but to be honest there's nowhere I'd rather be on a bitterly cold January morning than the sidelines of an under-21 club championship match. Even watching on as swarms of under-7s and under-8s run around the local club field on a Saturday morning isn't a chore.

It's more than just a love for the games themselves, I reckon. It's a passion for all the things they represent. More than that, even, it's a lifestyle choice. I'm sure there's many a 'GAA widow' out there who can attest to just that.

Back in college I'd luckily picked up a bit of work for the local newspaper reporting on the local club. It was a handy few bob but, to be honest, I'd nearly have done it for free. I attended most of the games they wanted me to cover anyway, always spotting the same 'aul fellas' on the line each week – whether it be at a senior football league game in Swords or an under-16 camogie challenge in Sandyford. I suppose it's a very Irish thing – the 'well, I was actually at the game' defence when offering an alternative point of view on the weekend's action at the clubhouse bar on a Sunday night. I had the opportunity to offer such opinions in print each week and I loved it. But I wanted more. At 23 years of age and just finished college, I was burdened with itchy feet and blessed in equal measure with an as-yet-untainted credit history.

Outside of my desire to travel, though, I was genuinely intrigued that something so intrinsically Irish as the GAA could be prospering in lands so far away. They didn't teach all that much about the Irish emigrant community when I was at school and it wasn't something that had ever really occurred to me before, to be honest. But with the appetite now well and truly whetted, I wasn't long in convincing myself that this mind-bogglingly huge journey I'd thought up was just about the best hare-brained scheme I'd ever devised. I was all psyched up and ready to go. Now for the details.

It was hard to know where and when to start. The only thing you can ever really be sure of in a GAA calendar year is that the two All-Ireland finals will be played on the first and third Sundays in September. Even that can be subject to change. So the plan became pretty simple. I'd leave the day after the All-Ireland football final of 2007 and I'd be back in time for the following year's decider in Croker.

The next task was to figure out where exactly I'd be going. Despite the obvious desire to go absolutely everywhere, it soon became apparent this was going to cost me a small fortune. I would hit as many major cities as I could, I decided, and from there I'd try to see as many of the surrounding places as I could.

So there I am, ticket in hand, bags packed and butterflies hurling in my stomach at Dublin airport. The last act on Irish soil had been to watch the All-Ireland football final. Kerry, beaten Munster finalists, knocked the stuffing out of a shell-shocked Cork team. Typical. It would be a bloody miracle, I remember thinking to myself, if I'm sitting here this time next year and anyone other than Kerry have Sam locked away in the glove compartment.

Visas in order, vaccinations received, money changed and laptop charged. I'm off around the world in GAA days. First stop: Dubai.

ASIA

1

THE CRADLE OF GAELIC CIVILISATION

MONDAY, 17 SEPTEMBER 2007 – DUBAI

It was late summer as I landed in Dubai International Airport and bloody roasting – 4 a.m. local time and about 45 degrees outside, and that at the very *end* of their summer. I could only imagine how hot it was in July.

Part of the plan when I set off on my little adventure was to 'learn by doing'. I hoped to learn as much about each place as I could, completely on my own – no *Lonely Planet*, no advance hostel bookings and no notion of what to expect until I landed in each city's respective airport. All I'd have with me was an onward plane ticket and a number for a lad in the local GAA club. In many cases all I'd end up having was the plane ticket. This sounded great in pre-game theory, but I was almost immediately forced into a rethink. First pitch, first strike. I hadn't factored into the equation the Muslim holiday of Ramadan. And I'd landed right in the middle of it.

My Indian taxi man, a jovial Hindu character named Mohinder, laughed as he told me how hot it had been the week before. Turns out it was over 50 degrees at one point. Crazy stuff. With my big Paddy head on me, I was an easy mark for Mohinder and ten minutes later I found myself in an Indian hotel in the city. Of course, I'd later learn it was his family's hotel and, as such, the guy hadn't even been a taxi driver. The place wasn't too bad, to be fair. But there was something seriously amiss in the city. It was early on

15

a Monday morning and the road was completely empty the whole way from the airport.

I'd expected Dubai to be quite Western-orientated, yet somewhat Arab-leaning. A liberal paradise in the middle of the Gulf. I'd never really thought to check, to be honest. I knew the place was full of Europeans and North Americans, but the last thing I expected was Islamic law. Turns out, for the entire month nothing is allowed to pass your lips while the sun is in the sky. No smoking, no drinking, no eating.

Mohinder's aunt Deekha explained that this Ramadan business was actually great for her and the rest of the Indian community, as the Muslim contingent just didn't come out in the daytime. For an entire month, the world was their oyster.

Nervous, to say the least, I reckoned I'd better not venture too far lest the nagging desire for lunch hit me at an inopportune moment ... I imagined myself staring out from a Dubai jail cell for munching on a bag of Taytos. Deciding to play it safe, I found refuge in the only place I was sure to solicit some sound advice. A short nap later, and the worst of the midday sun past, I set off for the closest Irish bar Google Maps could find me. The Irish Village.

Ten minutes after flagging down a cab I arrived to find the Village was actually built into the side of the Dubai tennis stadium complex. There were old-style wooden alcoves inside, but most importantly for my purposes it was full of Irish staff. It turned out the place belonged to an Irish businessman named Colm McLoughlin, the head of the Dubai Duty Free and president of the Dubai Celts GAA Club. I also soon found out that this was the real heart and centre of the Irish community in Dubai, just as would prove to be the case with so many other Irish bars in cities around the world. It had been the go-to place to watch the All-Ireland final the previous Sunday, for example, but all was a little quieter than usual since Ramadan had only just begun. As I said, during the Muslim holy festival, which, like Easter, moves from year to year, there is no alcohol allowed between sunrise and sundown. The sun was still in the sky but I was parched. Bummer.

For the rest of the year, Dubai's nightclubs and trendy bars thrive. Festivals are regular occurrences here, too, and only a few weeks before my arrival the Irish Village had held one of its biggest. The preparations for the pub's annual beer festival (the ideal way to stock up for the dry month ahead) had seen a massive air-conditioned tented arena erected over two of the tennis courts that run outside its front door. With a massive 40-foot screen, nests of tables and miniature stadium terraces in each of the four corners, it must have been a sight to behold. The management had decided to leave the tent and screens up following the festival's end for the All-Ireland final and the Rugby World Cup. It really seemed to be the ideal place to watch a match. Unless, of course, you happen to be a Corkman and that match is the 2007 All-Ireland Senior Football final.

Gasping for the bliss of air conditioning, I quickly propped myself up at the bar inside the door. It wasn't long before the oddness of the situation I was in really hit me. Surrounded by ashtrays, this place – at least in the daytime during Ramadan – was the exact opposite of Ireland. Here you had to come indoors to have a pint, a smoke and cool down. In Ireland, just the opposite. You'd be beaten out the door, fined and cursed from on high for the very same.

I was not long in my seat when a barman came up to say hello and take my order. We got to chatting. Turned out his name was Dermot Brazil and he'd spent the last few years playing intermediate hurling for the Craobh Chiaráin club in Dublin. Small world.

Coincidentally, I'd been in Chiaráin's clubhouse at Parnell Park just before I'd left to watch their senior hurlers get beaten by Lucan Sarsfields in a club championship game. That evening I'd spotted a Dubai Celts GAA club jersey hanging on the clubhouse wall. I'd lodged it to memory. Now it was all beginning to make sense.

Teams from the two clubs had played each other the year before in a challenge and I was directed towards a small crystal jug in the corner of the Village bar. A thank you, it read, from the members of Craobh Chiaráin to the Dubai Celts GAA club. Halfway around the world and it felt like I'd barely left.

At that point there were about seven staff standing having a chat and I was one of only three or so people in the entire bar. The place had only opened up at around six o'clock. Needless to say I had several questions about this curious bar staff-to-clientele ratio. At about seven o'clock, another three barmen walked in to start a shift. I was really confused. The explanation turned out to be quite a simple one, though. Sundown had been predicted for 7.04 p.m. Sure enough, come 7.03 p.m., the queue was nearly out the door. The place was jam-packed with thirsty Irishmen and fellow expats from the Western world over.

The national lines tend to blur in these expat communities and you soon find that you ultimately have far more in common with your neighbours back home than you have to fight about. One of the fun parts of tribal banter comes through sport, and with the Rugby World Cup just having started in France the week before there was plenty of it. Scotland were due to take on Romania a few hours later and my new Chiaráin friend was chock-a-block with orders, so I planned to take in the air-conditioned sanctuary of the tented village, its giant screens and beanbag couches a fairly tempting prospect with the heat still in the 30s outside.

I was at the bar and about to order a final beer to take with me out to the tented oasis when I noticed a familiar-looking face beside me. I tapped the man on the shoulder out of pure curiosity. I was full sure it was Jeremy Guscott. I wasn't far wrong. Five hours later, me and Gary, brother of the legendary English rugby centre and BBC commentator, are falling out of the giant tent celebrating a Scottish win, most of which neither of us really remembered the following morning. Gary still played the odd game of rugby, I do recall him telling me, though, and he'd dabbed a hand at Gaelic football in his time, too. Hurling, however, was where he drew the line. The rest of us were just plain lunatics, in his mind.

It had been a hectic start, but a tremendously enjoyable one, and I surmised that the Irish Village would be a place whose door I'd darken some time down the road again. I was sad to learn, however, that the building itself was due to be knocked down. The tennis stadium, into the side of which the bar is built, was being levelled to make way for a new hotel. All the other main sports stadiums in Dubai are being moved to a new site just outside the city, to a paradise named Sports City, which is currently under construction. An equally enticing new theme park called Dubailand is also being built, I was told. It seemed nothing was ever finished in Dubai.

My opening night had been productive in more ways than one. I had acquired a few contact numbers for the lads in the local GAA club and I soon set about making some calls in the hope they'd be free for a bit of chat while I was in town. Luckily, they were. I was to meet the chairman and vice-chairman of the Dubai Celts across the city the following evening.

TUESDAY, 18 SEPTEMBER 2007

Daithí Hanley and Donal McCarthy were busy knocking heads in the coffee shop of the city's Crowne Plaza Hotel as I walked in the door. I was scouring around for the two most Irish-looking heads I could see in the room and thought I'd spotted them pretty quickly. Unsure, however, I adopted a position at an adjoining table – I was trying to confirm their identities through the wonderful magic of the Irish accent. It soon became evident they were Corkmen, but their heads were down in the business at hand and they hadn't noticed my arrival. It soon became apparent, too, that this was actually a committee meeting I was listening in to. Being a Dub, I held my breath. I was quietly hoping that I might be let in on some big secret. GAA meetings are never that glamorous.

The second annual Gulf Gaelic Games festival was now just four months away and the lads were up to their eyeballs in organisational matters. In January 2007, the Celts had welcomed the football All Stars to the city, an event that had brought the curtain down on the inter-county careers of Kerry legend Seamus Moynihan and Tyrone star Peter Canavan. Alongside the big game itself, though, the Celts had also hosted the biggest-ever Gaelic Games festival to be held in the Middle East. Twenty-six teams, from Ireland to

Bahrain and England to Abu Dhabi, had played in over seventy games at all four codes. In what had been quite the international event, the Limavady Wolfhounds had beaten Hong Kong in the men's football final, Fulham Irish had won the football shield and St Brigid's of Dublin had beaten the hosts in the hurling final. Proper international honours list, that one. In 2008, they were aiming even higher.

I soon plucked up the courage to waltz over and say hello. Sentences had stretched to intervals of 30 seconds apart, so I surmised the meeting had ended and that I would no longer be intruding on matters official. I was invited to sit down, and I got the impression they were both confused and intrigued as to just what I was up to on my mad sojourn around the world. It wasn't long, though, before the lads started waxing lyrical about the huge event they were working so hard towards. Club chairman Hanley, a Gaelgeoir from Kerrypike just outside Cork city, and vice-chairman McCarthy, from Carrigtwohill, an uncle to Cork hurler and former All Star Niall, were hoping to eclipse the success of that first event in 2007. They planned to welcome 30 teams to the Dubai Polo Grounds for what would be the biggest international GAA sevens tournament in the world. The work was well under way, but there was still much to be done.

McCarthy was about to get to toiling on the invitations, and Hanley was heading back to Ireland in a few days to update Croke Park on how things were progressing. He'd also been charged with the task of picking up some hurls and sliotars while he was there. They don't grow on trees in Dubai, you know. Very little does.

It wasn't just the Gulf Games that were coming back to Dubai in 2008, though. The All Stars were coming back, too. But this time it was the ladies' football All Stars. TG4 were on board to film the weekend's action and sponsorship from a host of local businesses had already been secured. All the parts were thankfully beginning to slot nicely into place. This was the biggest event in the GAA calendar in the Middle East. It was an annual event crucial to the success of the Celts.

There are several other GAA clubs in the Gulf. Abu Dhabi Na Fianna, Clann na hOman and Kuwait Harps, plus the Qatar and Bahrain GAA clubs, are all thriving, but as the Celts are by far the biggest club in the region it was important to them to get meaningful games against stronger teams from outside the Middle East. A victim of their own success, to a degree, the Celts also had the largest pick of players and thus usually had the strongest teams at all four codes. They were just too good for most other clubs in the Gulf, so tough and testing games were hard to come by. Considering their relative distance from any other similarly sized GAA club, their success at a competitive level had been remarkable. In 2007, at the All-Asian Gaelic Games festival – in which the Celts were usually the only representative from the Gulf region – Dubai had enjoyed unparalleled success. They won the ladies' football tournament and the men's B football event, and McCarthy's own charges claimed the continental hurling crown ahead of Hong Kong in the inaugural year of the small-ball competition. Kings of all Asia!

The Asian Games are a once-a-year event, however, and a club like Dubai need more than that to keep their players interested. Equally important was maintaining the support of the general community. In that regard, the 2007 All Stars visit had been a huge success for the club. Over 4,000 spectators had come out to watch the game itself, and RTÉ personalities Michael Lester and Micháel Ó Muircheartaigh had also travelled over from Ireland to offer a hand. Ireland's greatest living commentator even lent his talents on the commentary for every game of the day, including the smaller warm-up games. Indeed, testament to the man and his almost unrivalled popularity among the GAA fraternity in Asia (former GAA president Seán Kelly does give him a run for his money), he even spent the early part of the day learning stories about local players and their families and any other funny titbits he felt might be useful. The event proved a huge success for all concerned and was a big boost for the GAA in the region. The games are only relatively young there, but they're growing up fast.

AROUND THE WORLD IN GAA DAYS

The Gulf was actually the birthplace of Gaelic Games in Asia, and McCarthy had been involved since the very beginning. It all started in Dhahran in Saudi Arabia in the 1980s. And it all started with hurling. A company called Masstock, with whom McCarthy had been working at the time, had a huge operation up and running there and the place was swarming with Irish expats. As so often happens when you get ten or more GAA heads in a room, the idea was soon hatched to set up an inter-firms hurling match within the company. From there, Ireland's most beautiful game began to blossom in the Arabian desert. The growth of hurling in the region was slow initially, but the seeds had been sown.

As the longest-serving GAA man out there, McCarthy recalled where it all began. The first-ever games of hurling were played in 1984 and 1985 with the inter-firms, he tells me, but then there was a gap of a few years. A lot of the projects within the company moved home and there weren't enough people left around to play against. It wasn't until 1991 that McCarthy hurled in the Gulf again.

'It was for Saudi Aramco against Kentz in Dhahran,' he recalls. 'Kentz were always big supporters of the GAA out here, and one of their directors, Noel Kelly, in particular. He would have hurled with Kentz in that game in 1991. There was skin and hair flying everywhere that day. I actually got a bad knock over the eye myself and I ended up having to go to the hospital. The law in Saudi at the time said that you had to report any injuries to the police, so I ended up going into the hospital through the back door. A girl from Clare, who was a doctor there at the time, stitched me up. We ended up going out drinking with her afterwards!' Mustn't have been Ramadan. Either way I got the impression McCarthy wouldn't have struggled to track down a bottle of brandy.

A year later in Dhahran, McCarthy, alongside fellow Corkman Johnny Rea, founded the first-ever GAA club in the Middle East – the ingeniously christened Naomh Abdullah's. The numbers of Irish were huge in the Gulf back then, according to McCarthy, and many of those would have been GAA men. The competition was intense and the particularly strong team from Almarai (a company

that also happened to be packed to the gills with Irish employees at the time) would have been intense, too. But things change. There was a mass exodus a couple of years later, which led McCarthy, and the core of the GAA in the Gulf region, to Dubai and the beginnings of what now stands as the biggest club in the region.

The Dubai Celts were eventually set up in 1995 by Paul Beecher and Paul McCabe, both of whom have since returned home to Ireland. Unfortunately, the Celts' progression can largely be tied into the demise of Abdullah's. The rapidly changing social climate in Saudi Arabia led many Irish families away from the country, and Dubai offered an ideal haven. So the Celts went from strength to strength, as Abdullah's devolved into nothingness.

It was getting late by the time I left McCarthy in the bar of the Crowne Plaza. I was looking ahead to my final day in Dubai, which, despite all its frills, really hadn't got all that much to offer at that time of year. There *was* one building that had taken my fancy, though, and I headed straight for that first thing in the morning.

WEDNESDAY, 19 SEPTEMBER 2007

It wasn't hard to see why there were more than 4,000 Irish nationals living in Dubai, from teachers and doctors to banking officials such as Hanley and business consultants such as McCarthy (he travels a lot with work and, incidentally, also founded the Clan Na nGael hurling club in Atlanta back in the 1990s). For people who call the city home, the place has everything they could ever want. For visitors, however, especially during September, the world-renowned and stunningly beautiful Burj Al Arab hotel is one of the few attractions. Outside of its fame as the world's first seven-star hotel, it also illustrates just how ingrained the Irish are in all aspects of the international communities in which they reside.

Stunning 'spitting' fountains in the hotel lobby greeted me as I walked in the door. There were aquariums alongside the escalators, gold-rimmed elevators and a view of the massive replica world map being built in the form of large islands just offshore. The Burj is meant to look like a sailboat, and in the foreground of its view sits the equally stunning Jumeirah Beach Hotel, built in the shape of a wave. You can work out where they were going with the concept. (If you're looking for directions, you can't miss it. It's just down the road from the indoor ski slope that sits proudly next door to one of the city's biggest shopping centres.)

With the most touristy look on my face I could muster, I marched proudly up the long gangway that led to the main entrance and walked straight through the lobby doors. Unaccosted by security, I even managed to make it to the top floor in the lift, where I was greeted by the ongoing construction of the giant offshore islands. (A local travel agent would later swear blind to me that David Beckham had already purchased Canada.) It was all a bit surreal. However, most incredible to me was what I learnt while I was on my way out the door. The hotels, it seems, are both run by a Galway city native named Gerry Lawless. One year later, almost to the day, I'd meet his brother, Billy, in the bar he owns in Chicago. You really just can't get away from us Irish anywhere.

It isn't just the incredible level of influence the Irish seem to wield over these places that runs as a common thread internationally; it's also the relationships the GAA enjoys with other sporting organisations. In Dubai, for example, the Celts are tenants of the Dubai Exiles Rugby Club, based just south of the city beside the camel racing track. The Dubai Dingoes Australian Rules team also share the ground and the two clubs regularly test each other at their respective codes, as well as the odd venture into compromise rules. In fact, in Dubai some months later then GAA president Nickey Brennan would sit down with AFL chief Andrew Demetriou to revive the International Rules series between the two countries.

The Celts' relationship with the Exiles was a healthy one, but it was expensive – they were paying €5,000 per year in rent. Having a place to call their own would be just what the doctor ordered. Sports City, McCarthy hoped, could offer his club the chance to have just that. Hopefully, should I ever return, I'd be able to enjoy a daytime pint in the new Irish Village built into the side of the GAA stadium in Sports City. Well, stranger things have happened.

Ideally, I would have liked to go everywhere in the Gulf on my little trip. Unfortunately, it proved just plain impossible, both logistically and financially. Clubs have been popping up all over the area in recent years and the list of places to go wasn't short or uninteresting.

One place that certainly sounded fun was up the road in Oman. It wasn't really somewhere you'd expect to find a GAA club, but, just like an oasis in the desert, sure enough, one had popped up where you'd least expect it. In the capital city of Muscat, Clann na hOman GAA club have been gathering strength since their foundation in 2003. They took a huge leap forward in 2007, when they officially signed up under the umbrella of the Asian County Board – the governing body of the GAA in Asia. Some months later, Kuwait and several other clubs followed suit.

Terri Johar, the president of the Irish Society in Oman (of which there are around 150 members), and fellow expat Colin Butler had come together and invited members of the society to a kickabout at the Al Swadi Hotel four years earlier and from there the club was born. After months of training on the front lawn of the hotel, with numbers increasing all the time, the club had finally decided to take the leap forward and ask the local rugby club for the use of their grounds. The rugby boys duly obliged, and from there the club has gone from strength to strength. Clann teams still regularly travelled to the United Arab Emirates to take on their neighbours, and the Celts in Dubai were actually preparing to welcome Abu Dhabi Na Fianna and Clann na hOman the following Friday. I was ruing the fact that I wasn't going to be around.

The Gulf Gaelic Games and the highly regarded Bahrain tournament offer opportunities for clubs in the region to stretch their legs, but in reality expat communities need to work together to properly manage resources. In 2007, Clann na hOman succeeded in keeping an Aussie Rules team running all year long. The story is much the same for the clubs of Kuwait and Qatar, who also travel to take on their nearest rivals in blitzes and tournaments every few months that keep the appetite for competition high. One of the bigger of these tournaments in the Middle East is the one in Bahrain and it's an event renowned as much for its craic as for its football. It sounds like something that would be right up my street. Sadly, my time in the Gulf was short. I had a date at the All-China Gaelic Football Games two days later.

2

THE ALL-CHINA GAMES

'One day, in the year 2006, the Lord looked down at the land of north-east China and was well pleased. He soon realised something was missing, however. Finally, it came to him. With a great roar, he summoned the Archangel Michael. "Mick," he bellowed, "did you know that there is not one Jaysus GAH club in the whole of shaggin' north-east China?" . . . Thus was the seed of divine inspiration planted in the hearts of selected Irishmen to begin a Gaelic football team in Dalian, the better to ease the hardship of their emigrant lives in a land far away from the misty bogs and TK red lemonade.'

– The Gospel according to the
Dalian Wolfhounds GAA Club

Whatever little I knew about Dubai on landing there, I knew even less about my next port of call. In fact, I'd never even heard of the place until I came across it as the host city for the All-China Games. Dalian is probably best described as being level with Beijing and sandwiched between the Mongolian and North Korean borders. Roughly. It's actually closer to North Korea than anywhere else, but it's still very much mainland China. It's the kind of place I'm sure I would never have seen in my life under any circumstances had it not been for this book and the determination of one Meath man to start a GAA club there. The Dalian Wolfhounds were hosting the All-China Gaelic Games festival and I was going there to see it. Chance can be a fine thing.

I landed at Dalian airport after a highly efficient transfer through Beijing. Much to my surprise, I had my passport stamped and my pre-ordered visa approved with very little fuss. A far cry from the traumas of London Heathrow. From there, I left the small regional airport and with relief spotted a line of cabs queued up outside. This All-China Gaelic football championship was the one major event I had known about before I left Ireland. I'd been in touch with a couple of the lads at the Asian County Board before I left, just to get some details on the upcoming tournament. They had put me in touch with the main man there, with whom I'd then exchanged a few emails just to let him know I was coming and he had kindly booked me a room in the hotel where the six visiting teams planned to stay. To say he'd been accommodating would be a serious understatement. I'd have been lost without his help.

I had the name of the hotel written down in front of me as I climbed into the cab, but then came the culture shock. Dalian, unlike Hong Kong or Shanghai, or any other place that has felt the touch of a Western hand, wasn't exactly used to welcoming foreigners. Not to say the people were rude, or anything like that. Far from it, in fact. They just hadn't got a word of English between the lot of them.

After 40 minutes of frantic finger-pointing and what I'm sure was a highly offensive attempt on my behalf to correctly pronounce the phonetically scripted name of the hotel, we arrived at our destination. In giant letters, on the side of the building, was the phrase Sweetland Hotel. 'Oh, you mean Sweetland?' the taxi driver laughed. The phonetics of the Mandarin name for the hotel I'd been given didn't quite make sense to the taxi driver, it seemed.

Just happy to be there, I paid the driver and rocked up to the lobby. At reception, I was met with an even lower understanding of the English language. It was slightly frustrating but, in fairness, I'd be a little disconcerted if a Chinese guy came up to me in

Dublin and expected me to understand Mandarin. Luckily, help was at hand. The one-man All-China Games, Mikey Farrelly, came to my rescue after spotting the puzzled-looking lad in the GAA jersey scratching his head. That, and it felt like we were the only two white guys within a hundred miles.

Originally from Kells in Co. Meath, Farrelly had called the far north-east of China home for the last three and a half years. In 2004, he and his wife, Ava, moved from Dublin, where they met, to the city where she was born. Since then they hadn't looked back. In 2006, Farrelly, a former Meath minor who was on the bench for the 1992 All-Ireland minor final, decided to bring a little bit of home to the Far East. The Dalian Wolfhounds GAA club were soon born, and their finest hour hadn't been long in coming, with the honour (and stress) of hosting the All-China Games. The city had never seen the like.

The hotel was a plush five-star job without any sign of Western influence at all. Only a handful of the more than a hundred staff members in the hotel spoke any sort of English and the decor was as typically Chinese as you'd be likely to find anywhere. The place even boasted a mesmerising 'global village' (think Liffey Valley food court built with 15 restaurants from different countries in an indoor plastic forest). The place was bustling, as is normal for an economically booming hub, with the usual clientele of Chinese, Japanese and Korean businessmen, but there was something slightly different in the air that weekend. The Irish were coming.

The only other new arrival to have reached Dalian by that stage was GAA referee Pat McGovern, who had flown in all the way from his home in Galway. An inter-county official, he was enjoying one of the very few perks the men in black actually get outside of free advice from angry players. He was fresh as a daisy with excitement as Mikey introduced us, despite a hefty flight that had seen him come through Frankfurt and Seoul en route to north-east China. Mikey headed off to continue with his organisational duties, as Pat and I sat down for a beer in the lush lobby (it even boasted a koi-filled indoor pond!). He was excited about the weekend's activities ahead, but told me he had to leave straight away after the Games, as he was due to ref a Galway county semi-final the following weekend.

It wasn't long before he was on my case to ref a few of the games for him over the weekend. I insisted I would not be taking up any such offer, but he told me to sleep on it and let him know in the morning. It was only 10 p.m. or so, but we were both knackered. A long weekend lay ahead, for both of us.

FRIDAY, 21 SEPTEMBER 2007

After a coma-like slumber I awoke with golden sunshine beating through my tenth-storey window. The hotel phone was jumping off the hook. It was my new buddy Pat, suggesting I get out of bed and come for a wander around the city. I threw on a few clothes and met him in the lobby before we set off. Around the corner from the hotel two things caught our eye straight away. First, the Olympic square. The five Olympic rings on a kind of monument with five or six AstroTurf soccer pitches surrounding it were certainly eye-catching. Second, across from the pitches, where the action was oddly frantic even for a Friday morning, a massive David Beckham poster hung on the front of the local sports shop. They were soccer mad.

As we rolled up to the fences for a closer look, we noticed that there seemed to be two underground entrances at either end of the square, in and out of which hundreds of people were appearing and disappearing by the second. On further investigation, we found a three-storey shopping centre under there, and a McDonald's proudly plopped at the entrance to welcome you in. But this was northern China, where the Communist Party were supposed to be at their strongest. Giant corporate footballing icons, golden arches and underground shopping centres betrayed an uncomfortable truth that the Communist Party would be at pains to acknowledge. Their grip appeared to be loosening.

On our way back from the shopping centre we decided to walk by the sports shop for a closer look when we noticed a gang of locals gathered with what can only be described as tennis racquets. It turned out they were practising their routines for the Olympic opening ceremony. We were querying the fact that there were only about 30 people there as we took a peek around the next corner. What we thought was just a sports shop was actually the back of the Dalian Sports Stadium and it was packed to the gills with people doing laps and holding banners. A loud voice roared orders over the PA system, telling the masses where to go. Surreal, to say the least.

Pat and I had been getting funny looks all day, but hadn't taken much heed. As we left the stadium, though, a particularly bizarre moment caught us off guard. The schools had just finished for the day and local kids were flooding the square, with hordes of schoolgirls walking past giggling in our direction. Tends not to happen quite so much on Grafton Street. Apparently, as Mikey explained later that evening, Westerners are a rare sight in those parts. Apart from the 70-foot Beckham, of course.

We arrived back at the hotel shortly after escaping our adoring fans, still laughing about what we hoped was a case of mistaken identity – they probably thought we were movie stars or musicians, or whoever – and met Mikey. He'd been checking people in for the past few hours. The lack of English comprehension at reception was by now beginning to fray his nerves, too. Luckily, his wife was on hand to bail him out and share the load. We decided to leave him be and soon got chatting to a young couple we'd spotted on the other side of the lobby. Sporting a pair of Shanghai Saints GAA T-shirts, they'd just come from the local beach and had a story to tell from their morning that would leave the average Irish parent scarred for life. Splashing along in the sea, they had taken their eye off their blue-eyed, blond-haired little boy for two seconds only to turn around and see he was nowhere in sight. Panic had gripped for a second, but they then spotted the culprit marching up the beach with their child in his arms. He only wanted to 'borrow "it"', he explained. He had his family already lined up for a picture with the child. The inappropriateness of the situation was quickly explained to the genuinely confused local man and no grudges were held. Still, time to leave the beach, they reckoned. The couple explained to us that this kind of unwanted attention occurred a fair bit where they lived in Shanghai, but it was normally just pinching and groping on the subway – this was the first attempt to 'borrow' one of their offspring. Pat and I were beginning to wonder if *we* might have been kidnapped had we not fled the square when we did. Best not to dwell.

The lobby was now packed with GAA pilgrims queuing up to be checked in. Four women's football teams and four men's teams had gathered for the event and the atmosphere was building. The host team, the Wolfhounds, were the smallest club by a mile. Unlike most other GAA clubs around the world where the Irish populations are relatively large, Dalian boasts a very limited number of expats. Around 17 or so Irish people live there, Farrelly reckoned. It's rare in itself to learn that there's somewhere left in the world that the Irish haven't invaded in numbers, but in a GAA context the place was even more unique. Farrelly was one of just two Irish men that were members of the club. It boasts one of the most international spectrums of membership of any club in the world; players from as far afield as Australia and Mongolia called the club home (word of an Aussie Rules team being set up was already spreading while I was there).

The Wolfhounds were the hosts, though, and if there was one thing they did well it was organising a session. After everyone was checked in, word was put out as to where the festivities would be happening that night. A small student bar in the city was chosen for starters, and there people from all four clubs mixed at ease. Most of them knew each other anyway from previous China Games or Asian Games, but there were always new people landing from Ireland as business continued to boom. Concerns for match readiness ahead of the following day's tournament didn't seem to be high on the priorities list. Beer, and one other crucial subject, were holding everyone's attention: Ireland were playing France that night in the Rugby World Cup and no one seemed to know where, or even if, it was showing in Dalian. As you might imagine, it wasn't really a rugby town.

Proving that the world-renowned Irish ingenuity was still alive and well, someone had got hold of a place to watch the game and a fleet of taxis were soon dispatched. I don't think anyone was really prepared for what we found when we got there, though.

A queue of rugby-hungry Irishmen and women soon formed outside a rather inconspicuous-looking entranceway. It seemed a little odd, but in groups of four and five we were herded into the place, where we were presented with a tiny and pretty dodgy-looking lift. Up three floors we went, and the doors opened to reveal what can only be described as a Mongolian-themed strip club.

Scratching our heads as the lift closed behind us, we soon spotted a few of the party heading behind a large red drape, and all was finally revealed. Behind the magic curtain sat a tiny side bar, fairly Western in appearance and with Heineken on tap. A somewhat rare but nonetheless welcome novelty. More importantly, though, it had a big-screen television on the wall pumping in South African TV's live coverage of the game (weirdly, this was the only satellite feed they could get in Asia for the tournament). Thoughts of the next day's games seemed to be in the back of everyone's minds, but as Ireland threw away their World Cup dream people began to look around and realised that it was nearing four in the morning. The bus was due to leave from the hotel in four hours and the first game threw in at 9 a.m. Pat, I soon learned, had long since turned in for the night. With a sore head and a heavy heart at the scoreline in front of me, I soon saw the wisdom of his ways.

Time for bed. There was a championship in the morning.

SATURDAY, 22 SEPTEMBER 2007

I woke up with a pounding head. No phone call this time, though. I rolled around and grabbed the silent alarm clock, only to see it was 7.55 a.m. The bus was leaving in five minutes. Uh-oh. I looked out the window to see the sun beating down, as I scrambled to throw on a pair of shorts and a T-shirt, grabbed some cash and zoomed down to reception. Murphy's Law and all that, the bus was turning around the corner as I hit the main reception. No panic, though. Taxi. The pitch was about a ten-minute drive away from the hotel in a place called Red Flag Park, which was primarily the home of a local soccer club. It was as fine a field as you'd find in any club in Ireland – minus the goalposts, of course. Farrelly had to get those flown in especially, with the aid of Shanghai GAA club. From there, though, they'd turned a fine plot of land into a GAA Mecca for the weekend. It really was a sight to behold.

I rolled up to pitchside as the first game was coming to an end. Shenzhen had lost to Shanghai in the men's senior football, and two ladies' teams had now taken the field to begin the second game. It was sevens football, so the numbers weren't all that vast, but the sideline was still packed with eager fans and players. The heat was beginning to take its toll on the several hungover heads drooping around the sidelines, and many had sought refuge beside the Guinness stand behind the far goals. For the most part, though, teams were taking shelter under the large tent that had been erected to protect them from the sun. There I found Joe Perrott, a young man from Aghabullogue in Cork, whose ear I was sure I had burnt near clean off the night before. He was only 24 years old but was the chairman of the Shenzhen Celts.

Before I knew what was happening, I was thrown a jersey and had been invited to play in the team's next game. Already one game down in the group stages, they needed to win the next two to have any chance of making the cup (or A-grade) final. At this stage, I was panting with dehydration, but with the figure of Pat McGovern veering down on me, spare whistle in hand, I happily obliged and threw on the jersey. Sheep as a lamb.

The opposition for my first game was the host side, Dalian. Incredibly, despite the intense heat and aching livers, the game turned out to be one of the most exciting I'd been involved in for quite a while. Heavily behind at half-time, we looked dead and buried, but in the second half we managed to pull ourselves back into it. Farrelly, clearly the best player in the ground on the day, single-handedly destroyed us from midfield, but the heat, and the fact that the poor guy probably hadn't slept in a month, got to him. From there, we came back. Our gigantic American full-forward Greg Schultheis rattled home a couple of goals and but for a last-minute strike from the Wolfhounds we would have won the game. It finished a draw. We'd have to beat Beijing in our last game to have any chance of making the final.

We would go on to do just that, but other results wouldn't go our way. Dalian, and the seemingly unstoppable Shanghai, won through to the cup final. Our day wasn't over yet, however. We still had a chance at silverware if we could beat Beijing in the Bowl (or B-grade) final. Game on, Ger.

It's amazing how you can get so sucked up in these things. A few hours earlier I'd been veering towards the Guinness stand for a cure, now I was lining out in a kind of county final with a medal at stake. GAA people seem to transform when there's a medal up for grabs. It's not just me. The whole Shenzhen team seemed to lift themselves in the kind of way where 60–40 balls become 40–60 balls, and personal safety is an afterthought.

Local television was on hand to cover the event, and a report on the evening news was even beamed into a few million homes that same night. In fact, when I'd first met Mikey in the hotel lobby he'd just come from a television interview promoting the event. He was busy doing another interview on the sidelines as we fought tooth-and-nail for an All-China Games men's football Bowl title in the background. A few weeks later I received an email with a link to CCTV, the television station in question. It showed Mikey chatting away about the merits of Gaelic football while in the background I was getting completely creamed scrambling for a breaking ball. Unfortunately – and suspiciously, I'm sure you'll soon be thinking – they didn't pick up any footage of me rattling home a ripping goal to the top corner inside the last five minutes. Typical. It didn't really matter at that stage anyway; the game was won. As the final whistle went, I remember thinking to myself that this was surely one of the strangest things I was ever likely to experience in my life. Our captain and goalkeeper, a Taiwanese-born American by the name of Sean Chang, went up to accept the All-China Games men's football Bowl trophy. Stranger than fiction.

Celebrations quickly subsided (for the time being) and we turned our attentions to cheering on our ladies' football team in their final. The Shenzhen Celts had joined forces with Dalian for the weekend and, in an exciting clash, they beat Beijing B in the Bowl final. The Shenzhen and Beijing men's teams lined the sideline with pints of Guinness in hand. (One of the English-born members of the Shenzhen team had actually taken a nasty boot to the face and was drinking his pint from a straw through a hole in his bottom lip after just returning from the hospital.)

Beijing A eventually beat Shanghai in the ladies' Cup final, while in the men's final a hat-trick of goals from Davey Hayes, originally from the Good Counsel club in Dublin, led Shanghai to a deserved win over a gallant host side inspired by Farrelly. The winning Shenzhen men's team had three Americans in their starting line-up; the Dalian team boasted two Australians and two Chinese lads, as would the Shanghai Championship-winning men's team. This was international sport at its finest, folks. I think even Mícheál might have struggled with the commentary on some of those names, though.

It was 22 degrees when the first ball was thrown in at 9 a.m., and the heat had grown steadily until the final whistle was blown at 3.15 p.m. Pat McGovern had been out in the heat all day for every game without fail, and although the games provided a welcome break from the serious business of refereeing Tommy Murphy Cup finals and the like (he'd refereed Wicklow's epic win over Antrim in the Murphy Cup final a few weeks before), he was as tired as anybody. Ultimately, though, his efforts were just as valuable to the success of such an event as anyone's.

With the action ended and the winners' trophies presented to the captains, it was back to the hotel to get ready for the night's gala presentation banquet. The toilet facilities for the day had been two squatter Portaloos in the corner of the ground. With the burning sun beginning to set, the job of removing them didn't exactly strike you as the most appealing. Some sort of large truck would come along and pick them up, you might think. No such luck. A small Chinese man rocked up with a cart.

With the help of two other lads, he eventually got the cabins on board and began to heave the mass of mess towards the entrance gate. He hit a grate along the path and the loaded cabins began to rock ominously to their sides. The Irish nation in north-east China at that moment collectively held its breath. There are some things I'm sure people living there will always miss from home. Be grateful for your bogroll, lads.

Thankfully, the worst hadn't come to pass and the spectacle lost its allure by the time the two buses had arrived to take the eighty or so players and mentors to the most unusual venue ever conceived for a GAA medal ceremony. A sight, and a night, that I doubt will ever leave my mind.

The bus pulled up at the Sweetland Hotel at around 8 p.m. to take everyone to the banquet. Genghis Khan's Mongolian Barbecue was a 20-minute drive from the hotel in a place called Labour Park. Built in the shape of a giant football, it's one of the oddest sights imaginable in the centre of a downtown park. If you ever go to Dalian, or come across a holiday brochure for the place, it's the first thing you're likely to see. Even more mesmerising is the sight inside it.

The players filtered in and began to take their seats while I was still mesmerised, looking around. A bottle of Jameson was provided for each table free of charge as part of a sponsorship effort from the company and a choice of Taiwanese, Korean, Chinese or Mongolian food was available from the buffet counter. On the way up to watch your meal being cooked, you must first negotiate a rotating floor, and it was only when I was sitting down to eat that I realised the walls were actually made of water. Inside two of them bikini-clad female scuba divers were doing laps. And this was before the first bottle of Jameson had been cracked open.

About an hour later, fed and watered, a bizarre entertainment spectacle soon greeted the audience, who were still rotating around the stage. A kind of duet karaoke performance, complete with dancers. I reckoned I was just beginning to get my head around what was actually going on when the whole thing came to a sudden halt.

The Jameson had now well and truly been popped, and it was time for the presentation ceremony. The Irish Ambassador to China, Declan Kelleher, had flown up from Beijing to present the medals. It felt strangely rewarding to be standing there on stage, but no less bizarre. I really couldn't have imagined, six days after leaving Dublin airport, that I'd be standing in a giant revolving football with half-naked swimmers in the walls receiving an All-China Gaelic Games football medal from the Irish Ambassador to China. What a difference a week makes.

It all flew by like a daze and, with the presentations over, it was down to the serious business. Several of the teams had already headed for the next watering hole, but the Shenzhen lads and lassies had remained behind to polish off the rest of the Jameson. The craic was picking up by the minute, and some impromptu Irish dancing had broken out on the by then evacuated stage – the sound of *Riverdance* roared through the speakers. The bouncers, who were left completely baffled by what they were seeing in front of them, surely thought all Irish people were stone mad. It soon became obvious it was time to leave.

Luckily, a plan was afoot.

Making sure to stay in close proximity to a Chinese speaker (most foreign workers who are lured to work in China are provided with language classes), I queued with the others outside for a taxi. Next stop, Irish bar. Well, sort of. The Tin Whistle Pub in the city was formerly owned and run by an Irish man, but shortly before we arrived in Dalian the bar had been bought out by a local Chinese woman. The place had retained the name, but Dalian GAA's de facto clubhouse had since moved on (the Wolfhounds still sport the jerseys the bar sponsored a few years previously, though). It mattered little who owned the place to the visiting hordes.

The Shenzhen crew, armed with the remains of the leftover bottles of Jameson tucked under our jumpers, strolled in last to join the party, which was now in full flow. Had the place still been Irish-owned, you get the feeling they might have been more suspicious of the number of drunken Irish people ordering cans of Coke all night. It was a field day for the Tin Whistle, though, all things said. With such a limited number of expats in the city, I wondered how the bar survived there at all. I soon learned that Intel had already begun construction of a new factory and so my fears for the bar's future duly lessened.

The pub itself was split in two, into the front and the back (smokers') section. Both had ballads belting out through their rafters into the small hours until the bar staff finally got sick of the noise and decided to call time. Luckily, our new favourite Mongolian spot was still open around the corner. It was destined to be a messy one.

Hours later, and the sun long risen, people were beginning to check out of the hotel. A group of about 20 diehards had stayed up through the night and made the hotel lobby the new home of Irish music in the north-east of China. The staff at reception had been looking at us with pure bemusement all night long, unsure what to do. Luckily, they didn't have to worry too much. The fuel tanks were now empty and it was time for bed. The party split quietly and everyone headed for the hay.

The Beijing element had been at the core of the craic and I agreed to meet them for a pint again some time soon. Just so happens I was flying to Beijing a few days later.

3

THE OLYMPIC CITY

The head had all but returned to normal after the heavy weekend in Dalian. Sunday was spent re-gathering the bearings and taking a final look around. It was actually quite a big city, when you saw it in the light of day. The population was somewhere around the five million mark, or so I gathered. Not huge by Chinese standards. Bigger than the whole of Ireland, all the same. It was actually sort of like the Disneyland of north China. Many Beijing residents go there on their holidays, it turned out. But it was no Magic Kingdom, in my mind. I had actually toyed with the idea of spending my last day across the border in South Korea. The port city of Incheon is only just across the bay and from there it would have only been a short hop to Seoul. The immigration regulations in China are quite strict, however, and as I was only on a 30-day single-entry visa even a day trip would have meant obtaining a whole new visa to get back in. In the end, I just decided to gather up my things and head for Beijing. Shouldn't exactly run out of things to do there, I reckoned.

I landed in the airport in Beijing for the second time, but it was the first chance I had to take in some air. Misty and foggy, it was like a leaf blower had been through the place. It was a warm and musty day, and the sun was somewhat blocked out by the layer of smog that wraps around the city like a blanket. The Olympics were due to be held there in less than a year, but

41

the language barrier was as bad there as it had been in Dalian. I picked up a map in the airport before going anywhere near the taxi rank. I was trying to figure out roughly where I was headed, but the place is ridiculously big. I'd booked myself into a hostel in the downtown area before leaving Dalian so I would at least have a starting point. I was planning to stay for about two weeks, but I had nothing else booked, so was under no pressure. My next flight wasn't for a month and it was from Hanoi in Vietnam to Bangkok in Thailand. The plan was to get a train to Vietnam from Beijing. But those plans would change.

I eventually thought I'd figured out where I was heading, so hopped into a waiting taxi, pen-marked map in hand. The taxi man seemed to be delighted to have a white guy in his back seat and he happily smiled in feigned recognition of where I was asking him to take me. It didn't look that far on the map, so I thought it should be fine. Before we pulled out of the rank, he leaned over and turned on what I thought was the radio. Turned out it was an English-language instruction tape. City officials had sent out an edict to all the taxi drivers in Beijing: pass a basic English language exam before the Olympics, or lose your licence. If this guy was anything to go by (and the next 20 taxi drivers I met), there wouldn't be a single taxi left in Beijing come the opening ceremony.

We eventually rolled up at the hostel in the Chaoyang district of the city. It was right in the heart of downtown and in relatively close proximity to Tiananmen Square. I checked into my four-bed dorm and set out for a look around.

It soon became clear that walking anywhere in this city was completely pointless. The place is huge. There's a population of somewhere around twenty million and the urban part of the city has four main ring roads around it. Well, that's all they could fit on the map. My hostel was in the heart of the innermost square and to go from one side of that to the other took about an hour on a bike. To travel to the outer ring road would take about six, I figured. The sheer size of the place was quite simply mind-blowing.

The day was still young when I decided to rent a bike and take in as much as I could. Map in hand, I headed south towards some of the major attractions. I rolled through the Forbidden City and on past Tiananmen Square to the Temple of Heaven. The streets were scary. Although there are separate roads for bikes (there really are about ten million bicycles there), it's no less hazardous. Cyclists have their own separate traffic lights and everything, but it's not an easy system to comprehend, so the only safe path is to keep a local biker on your right and hope he doesn't get you killed.

The Forbidden City was as beautiful as pictures of it suggested, while Tiananmen Square was packed to the rafters with tourists. Down in the Temple of Heaven, however, I felt you could be anywhere in the world. An inner-city park of sorts, at its heart sits the Hall of Prayer for Good Harvest. No bikes are allowed inside the park, so it is one of the few places in the city that is genuinely peaceful. Even the smog feels less oppressive in there.

Beautiful ornamentations surround the hall. This is where the Chinese emperors used to be crowned and you really get that sense of history, as you stand there looking out at the surrounding city from up on top of the hill. The place is thousands of years old and there it was still standing proudly, safely lagooned away from the development that has changed the city that surrounds it. The main hall is architecturally magnificent and from an era long since past. It's also the emblem on the crest of the Beijing GAA club.

Night was beginning to descend on the city as I returned to the hostel. (I'd moved about two inches on my three-foot-by-two-foot map and it had taken me two hours to get there and two hours to get back.) There was an eclectic mix of Europeans and Americans in the hostel exchanging stories of the day's adventures in the city as I made it to base. One American was in the throes of recounting how she'd been taken in at Tiananmen Square by a local con artist. She and her husband had been invited to a local tea party by one of the rare English speakers in the city who had stopped them on the street and asked if he could practise his

English on them. An hour later they were in someone's house, drinking tea. Ten minutes after that they were getting charged the guts of US$300 for the pleasure. I couldn't help but snigger and enjoy my own sense of achievement at not having been killed, conned or mugged on my own little journey. I'd nearly been knocked down two or three times, but at least I hadn't spent a few hundred quid on tea.

I decided I deserved a beer as some reward but was conscious not to venture too far until I was sure I knew my way back. If you're lost there, you might as well be asking the trees for directions. So I took a little stroll up the side street next to the hostel. In that part of the city, everywhere looks like a slum from the outside. But that's not always the case inside. It's just that I was staying in the really old part of the city that had originally surrounded the home of the ancient emperors. If its walls could talk . . . Well, they probably couldn't speak English anyway.

Walking down the street, I spotted a white-looking head behind one of the bars and decided to nip in for a quick one. The bar was called Salut, and I assumed it was a French-owned spot. Three friends from Luxembourg ran the place, as it turned out, and it wasn't long before we got to chatting. They were out on the other side of the bar, swapping stories and telling me about life in Beijing. The place was so relaxed compared to the mayhem passing by its doors outside.

The lads had been there for two years and they loved it. The boss popped in and out every so often, so they tried to look busy every now and then. That night they were in particularly fine form, as their mate was visiting from home. The fellow visitor, Jean François – or Jeff, as he's known to his mates behind the bar – and I ended up polishing off an entire batch of the bar's home brew with three Irish girls we dragged in off the street.

If I thought the place looked foggy that morning, I'd know all about it 12 hours later.

THE OLYMPIC CITY

I awoke upside down at the wrong end of my bed in the hostel dorm. There was activity in the room, and I reached over to find my watch. It was only 8 a.m. Swedish tourists are definitely day walkers. Beijing, being more of a daylight tourist city than what I'd been used to, was like a paradise to them. That's not to say the place is unsafe or anything like that. Backpackers here just tended to like travelling in groups by day and sticking close to where they were staying at night. The language barrier there was still huge, too.

I was hoping to get away from the whole backpacker thing while I was there and solicit some local knowledge from those who call Beijing home. When in Rome . . . I'd been emailing Colin Saunders, a Dub from the Beijing football team, and although he was at work all day I'd arranged to meet him in the evening in a city bar. Should be fun. I was pretty sure he had been the last one to leave the hotel lobby in Dalian the previous Saturday night.

The day trips out of the city to the Winter Palace and the Great Wall had to be booked a day in advance, so I was forced to limit my explorations to more local attractions once again, as I passed the time before meeting up with Colin. I started across the street from the hostel at the closest McDonald's. I know what you're thinking. Did you really go all the way to China just to eat McDonald's? Well, no. But when you see the alternatives on offer, and the fact that you can't even decipher what's on the menu in half of these places, you quickly get over yourself. A Big Mac is a Big Mac, and there's a look-and-point system the locals have worked out with the tourists on the menu front. And it was obviously not just me. My map, which was just of 'urban' Beijing, had 96 McDonald's marked on it. It's hard to believe how recently there were people standing in front of tanks five minutes down the road.

Full of what I could only hope was beef, I headed across to the closest ancient amenity. The Bell and Drum Tower was an ancient temple of sorts (an American tourist would be stabbed to death there a year later during the Olympics), but its location, beside a McDonald's at a busy crossroads, summed up succinctly how much the city had changed. Temples and McDonald's and Luxembourg-owned bars side by side.

It occurred to me that I'd been in Beijing for a few days and hadn't come across sight or sound of anything Olympic-related, so I decided to head towards the Workers' Stadium, whose construction was much further advanced than many of the other stadiums further outside the city centre. It looked like a fine place, especially when compared to the relatively humble nature of its cousin in Dalian. I was highly curious about how people were going to get from place to place when the Olympics kicked off in ten months. McDonald's would certainly be busy.

The stadium was actually on the way to where I was supposed to meet Colin and, as time was getting away from me, I decided to make a beeline for the place where we were meeting up. I resolved to continue on foot, as it was actually much less stressful than shouting at taxi men who didn't understand the concept of left or right.

I ended up getting a little bit lost, but then noticed a few five-star hotels on the left side of the street and assumed these places often hosted Western tourists and businessmen, and so surely someone would be able to speak a little English and direct me on my way. Not on your life. Blank stares. The language difference was really beginning to take its toll on me. Even hand gestures were out. They only counted up to three on their fingers bizarrely, and enunciating any higher number required a two-handed gesture I hadn't quite mastered. I'd been trying to pick up some basic Mandarin, but it wasn't as easy as it sounded. The only piece of information that had stuck was that the Chinese phrase phonetically pronounced 'Mayo' quite literally translated into 'don't have'. Cue the childish giggles.

I eventually found my way and soon realised that all the Western bars were kind of lumped together around where most of the foreign embassies were based. No prizes for drawing the connection there. Oddly, there was no Irish bar there, though. There would be one established in time for the Olympics, of course (and when it opened,

Paddy O'Shea's would become a good source of support for the local GAA), but for now the local GAA folk hung out in a bar attached to a local youth hostel. It was called the Tree Bar and was hidden down a side street. There I found Colin sitting out with two other lads. One was Enda Brogan, a long-time resident of the city and one of the founding members of the Beijing GAA club. The other was RTÉ commentator Steven Aiken. Aiken was there for the week on a fact-finding mission ahead of the Olympics. He was a friend from home of Colin's family. Colin's job – he was one of the few Irish people I came across who didn't work for the Irish Embassy in one form or another – was largely hospitality-based. He looked after foreign clients and showed them around the city when they were visiting. There certainly seemed to be a market for foreign business visitors. A Hooters restaurant had just opened up around the corner.

Brogan had drifted somewhat away from the GAA side of things, he told me. He was now much more involved with the GAA's sister club Beijing Celtic, a local soccer club that was one of the biggest expat organisations in the city. He'd be back involved with the club by the time the year was out, though. The All-China Games were due in town the following June (the Games are normally held in June but had been moved in 2007 to accommodate the All-Asia Games, which had been held in Singapore). Indeed, Brogan would feature in an RTÉ news report on those Games, speaking on behalf of the Beijing GAA.

None of the lads at the table were really GAA men in the true sense, but that seemed to be a trend among many of the GAA clubs in Asia. You're never more Irish than when you're not in Ireland, it seems. Saunders was a soccer man, Aiken spent much of his time commentating on the Premiership and Brogan dedicated most of his efforts to Celtic. When it came to a shared interest and a common goal, however, everyone got together and pitched in. There were no such liberties as bans on foreign games that far from home.

People like Derry man Colin Dixon had been keeping the club going since its foundation as a men's football club back in 2003.

Since then they'd grown from strength to strength, and perhaps the biggest event for the club happened ahead of the 2005 All-China Games. A women's football team was established ahead of that tournament and since then the club had broken new ground. The first women's football team in mainland China, the Beijing GAA women's section, was now the largest international sports club for women in Beijing, a city with 20 million people in the urban areas alone. Aoife O'Loughlin, whom I'd met while she was pounding up and down the sidelines in Dalian the previous weekend, was one of the founders. Now, she was the chairperson of the entire club.

The real heart of the Beijing women's success had been their work in the community and their ability to bring local Chinese girls on board. In 2006, the Banshees, as they are known, didn't have a single Irish person on their A team. Aoife worked for the embassy, but unfortunately she wasn't around for the next few days. I got all the information I needed from the three lads in the Tree, though. Full of beer, I decided to head for the hills.

WEDNESDAY, 26 SEPTEMBER 2007

Once again I woke up arseways in a bed I am convinced was originally a cot. I was tired and restless and fed up, and I realised it was time to plan my next move. Two weeks would be far too long to spend in Beijing, and I wasn't short on options elsewhere. The only problem was that those options were somewhat problematic. Going to Japan (there has been a GAA club based in Tokyo since the mid-1990s and by the following year's Asian Games in Malaysia there would be a second one in the shape of the Kensai club) or Korea would be extremely expensive and I'd have to reorganise my Chinese visa all over again to get back into the country afterwards. Ditto Taiwan, the home of the late David Brady, after whom the men's senior football trophy at the Asian Games is named. Brady had been a driving force in the Taiwan club but had been tragically run down in Taipei a few years previously. I decided to make my next port of call somewhere more easily accessible.

I began to peruse the cheap flight websites at the hostel and see where I could head off to next. Shanghai was the early favourite. I'd been in contact with Ballymun native Noel Lennon from the Shanghai Saints and Sirens club in the weeks leading up to my departure from Ireland. He was also on the Asian County Board, and I'd been keen to meet him in Dalian. Unfortunately, he'd been dragged home to Ireland on another commitment that same weekend. (He would actually end up becoming the first-ever entrant into the Asian GAA Hall of Fame the following year in Malaysia.)

I checked my emails to see if he'd be back in Shanghai over the next few days, but unfortunately he wouldn't. Still, I thought, it's the closest place to Beijing and has a reputation as being a wild and fun city. An added bonus would be the fact that I wouldn't have to leave China and worry about getting another visa to get back in.

Just then I spotted a message in my inbox from Louise Weste of Shenzhen. There was a wedding coming up that weekend, she wrote, and I was invited to go along. They offered to put me up for a few days and show me around the place. It was hard to say no to an invite like that. Flights quickly booked for the following morning, room bill paid (I had to fork out for all five nights even though I'd only stayed for three, but even then it only cost a paltry €24), one more session in Salut to wave off Jeff and the lads, and farewells said to Colin et al. Next stop: Shenzhen, home of the 2007 All-China Games men's and women's Bowl champions.

4

THE SUNNY SOUTH-EAST

When I arrived in Shenzhen, I was convinced I'd left China altogether. At the exact opposite end of the country to Dalian, the place is sparkling and shiny new. It looked to me as if Beijing and the rest of the north was Communist-controlled, while Shanghai and everywhere south of it were much more Westernised. With a printout of the directions Louise Weste had given me, I climbed into a cab. The driver spoke English. Now, I was really confused. But equally delighted. I arrived outside the entrance to a downtown skyscraper at around 3 p.m. Home of the GAA in Shenzhen in more ways than one. A company called PCH International has its home office on the top floor and it was from there that the Celts took most of their members. Essentially an engineering company, it is owned by Corkman Liam Casey. It's no slouching operation, either. A few weeks later Casey was named the 2007 Ernst & Young Entrepreneur of the Year.

My host for the week was San Francisco native Josh Bizmanovsky, who had played corner-back for Shenzhen in Dalian the week before (quite the tenacious defender despite being a complete novice), and he was waiting to greet me at the Starbucks that sits next door to PCH. After a quick coffee, he took me upstairs to say hello to everyone in the office. There was quite a relaxed atmosphere, as offices go, but everyone working there is highly qualified and very good at what they do. Otherwise, I soon gather, they wouldn't be in south-east China working for a Corkman. Much of what they do centres around the massive factories that surround the city. There they make iPhones and other high-end technologies, and a lot of what the staff do is related in one way or another to that. It's a fine office, and the view is incredible. I hadn't been too hectic on the bearings front as I was shown around and this was just the tonic. Having been in Dublin, Dubai, Dalian and Beijing over the course of the last ten days, I was finding new geographical information somewhat tricky to process. It all became clear, though, once I had a proper look around.

'You see those buildings over there?' Josh asked me. 'Well, that's Hong Kong.'

Easy as that.

So, at least I had a rough idea where I was. Somewhat under the impression that Shenzhen was a sort of Hong Kong offshoot, the truth soon became apparent and Josh and I headed off to his apartment in a cab. Shenzhen is no suburb. In fact, the city has a population of around 12 million people all of its own. Its proximity to Hong Kong is no coincidence, though. Visa issues are just as prevalent in the lives of the people who live there as they are to tourists like me. While still a part of China, the option is there to head to Hong Kong by ferry (or by train) and thus reset your visa. Cunning in its simplicity.

Back at Josh's place, which was about ten minutes away by taxi, I quickly showered and got changed before we headed back to meet the rest of the lads from the club. We decided to get a quick bite on the way at the closest restaurant to Josh's apartment block. Yep, you guessed it: McDonald's. The look-and-point technique at the Golden Arches, which I had all but mastered in Beijing, had been keeping Josh alive for the few months that he'd lived there. A Big Mac is a Big Mac is a Big Mac.

It was after six as we returned to PCH. The office's local bar sits in a beautiful square in front of the main office block. It's called 3D and business had never been better since the Irish came to town. Meeting up with some old faces from the weekend before, I soon got to chatting with Joe Perrott once again. He was actually involved in a Cork under-21 hurling panel and was keen to get the small ball going in Shenzhen. Numbers, however, were obviously a major issue. He'd been having impromptu sessions with a few of the footballers and imparting his knowledge about the basics of the game to anyone who showed any interest. The target was to get a Shenzhen Celts hurling team together for the Asian Games the following year in Malaysia. The Celts' giant American midfielder, Greg Schultheis, was particularly keen on the hurling, it seemed. He'd been pucking a ball against a wall for months now in anticipation. Inside, I was smiling.

The youth of the club here was quite staggering. It was originally founded by Clontarf native Peter Lennon and a few others who had been part of a pioneering generation of young Irish professionals who had come to south-east China. Peter was now the president of the club, Joe the chairman and Louise the secretary. Not one of them over 30. A far cry from the old fogies in the boardroom you so often think of at home. They were excited to tell me all about the club they'd worked so hard to build, so finally I got around to asking them about the bar we were sitting in. Unsurprisingly, the GAA lads practically ran the place. Just like most other twenty-something professional Irish people abroad, they were fond of a few pints and the place had become a home away from home for them. The owner was a local Shenzhen man, but he couldn't have prayed for a better gang of people to adopt his bar as their own. When they first started drinking there, Joe and Peter told me, the place was like a wine bar. A little soulless, but handy, as it was so close to the office. Then, one night, the owner cornered Joe for an honest appraisal of what he thought of the bar and how it could be improved. With a few on him, Joe grabbed a beer mat, drew a bit of a diagram and suggested 'a few different types of beer and maybe a few stools or something'. A few weeks later the bar was gutted and completely renovated to the specs Joe had scribbled down. The owner wouldn't regret it, either.

AROUND THE WORLD IN GAA DAYS

I woke up in Josh's spare room and waltzed out into his sitting room, where we spent our second day on the trot watching television shows he'd downloaded from the US onto his laptop and whatever sport from America the local ESPN station had decided to filter in. We decided after a couple days of doing nothing that it was important to see the cultural side of the city, and not just the inside of the city's bars and the local McDonald's scene. Mikey Barry had been the character of the All-China Games the week before, but he hadn't been around for the past few days, so we decided to meet up with him and his wife that night for dinner. No better man.

Shenzhen is sort of a middle land in China, in that it's geographically located in between many of the main cuisines. Keen to get this point across, Mikey took us to a massive restaurant in a city centre shopping complex. Not having the strongest stomach, and fearing I'd end up ordering something lava-like by mistake, I left the ordering to the Corkman and his lovely wife. He'd been in Shenzhen for about eight years by then and his Mandarin was really very good. It was part of the package when you came to work in China that you took language classes, and Mikey was at the latter stage of that process, having progressed onto the written language – unquestionably, the most difficult to master. Thankfully, his wife spoke excellent English, too. Table etiquette is quite important in China and I was careful not to do something to offend the entire restaurant. The tables were round, and I was fumbling with the chopsticks, but the array of food in front of me was simply dazzling. There was seafood, chicken and beef. All the usuals. It seemed the restaurant specialised in bringing the best of Szechuan, Hotpot and all the other Chinese cuisines together. Being left-handed, I was already causing confusion at the table. Everyone in China is taught to eat with their right hand so as not to upset the reach of the person to their immediate left. The southpaw would have been beaten out of me long ago had I been Chinese, Mikey informed me comfortingly. Apparently, in a country where squat toilets are the norm and toilet paper exists only in Western hotels and residences, the left hand is used for something else entirely. I'll leave that to your imagination.

I wasn't quite sure what I'd actually eaten as I sat back after polishing off the final bite. It was very mild stuff, Mikey told me. Must take some getting used to. Between finishing dinner and leaving the restaurant, I'd succumbed to three bathroom visits. Josh, it seemed, after just a few months there, was already used to it. I'd only been in China a week, on the other hand.

After dinner and a few Alka-Seltzers, we headed off to a bar called Demon to meet up with the rest of the lads from the GAA. Although it was very Western-looking in layout and clientele, you would know you were still in China, but there was also all sorts of beers on tap and pool tables all around. The jukebox was blaring. In Shenzhen, karaoke is like a religion – a chain of bars called KTV had taken over there. Business executives from several large companies often spent their lunch breaks in those places, entertaining clients and such. I resisted the temptation. Big day ahead tomorrow.

SUNDAY, 30 SEPTEMBER 2007

Refreshed and at long last feeling somewhat human again, a big day lay in store for the Irish in Shenzhen. Eddie O'Sullivan's Ireland were on a mission of redemption back in France and the excitement was building in the south-east of China. We arrived early in McCawley's Irish Bar on Shekou Bar Street for a feast of Irish brekkie and a few warm-up beers. It wasn't the most regular haunt for most of the local expats there, but it certainly fitted the bill for certain occasions such as that one. It seemed every Irish expat in the city had converged there and it was still hours before kick-off. The NRL Grand Final (rugby league) between the Melbourne Storm and the Manly Sea Eagles was beaming through on the big screen. Next up, France demolished Georgia, and we knew our fate was in our own hands. We needed to beat the Pumas by eight points while scoring four tries for a bonus point in the process. We lost by 15.

I was beginning to think my presence in China had been some sort of curse on the Irish team. Then I remembered that I had actually been in Ireland for the Georgia and Namibia fiascos. Less said the better. We consoled ourselves with a few more beers and a bit of live music late into the night. We called it a night early enough, though; there was a wedding to go to in the morning.

MONDAY, 1 OCTOBER 2007

I was somewhat nervous about going to the wedding of a guy I'd only met very briefly, but Josh ran me through all I needed to know about Chinese ceremonies. I hadn't exactly planned for a wedding with a backpack stuffed full of rolled-up shorts and T-shirts, but was soon togged out with some of Josh's spare glad rags before we headed out the door. Josh was about a foot taller than me, so I was feeling a little like a 12 year old at his confirmation, rolling up to the bishop in his older brother's hand-me-downs. The wedding was taking place in a fancy downtown hotel and the hall was quite a sight to behold.

There are a few nuances with Chinese weddings (the groom was actually English and the bride a local Chinese girl) and the theme of this particular wedding was most definitely local, even though many of the guests were expats. We sat out in the lobby to have a few pre-reception drinks before we headed into the main hall. One of the things I still hadn't quite got my head around was Chinese customs. One of the most unusual of these is called a Hung Bao. Basically, instead of gifts, people attending a wedding will put money into a red envelope and hand it in at the door of the reception. That in itself isn't really all that strange (although it does feel a little like something from the *Godfather* movies). The strange part is that they take out the money and count it in front of you before marking down the amount you've given beside your name on the guest list. No room for skinflints. You'll be soon found out.

After my conservative donation was tallied in front of me, I got the nod and headed on into the banquet hall. It was a beautiful setting, as spectacularly adorned circular tables filled the room. I was sitting in the far corner with a few of the lads from the GAA team, so wasn't feeling too exposed. The ceremonies soon got under way, and it was quite the long and drawn-out ordeal. As half the guests were Western and half were Chinese, there were two MCs on the stage translating what was happening. The ceremonies were traditional and quite intriguing. There were about ten complicated rituals carried out involving the bride's father – one of them some sort of apple-biting thing – while a round of shots was sent to every table. Then, finally, it was down to the eating. Before we'd finished applauding the scenes on stage, a suckling pig had arrived on each of the tables. It was like something from a cartoon. I wasn't quite sure what to do with it.

It was a foetal pig, I was told, and you're only supposed to eat the skin. Far from foetal pigs at Chinese weddings I was reared. But I tucked in as part of my concerted effort not to stick out like a sore thumb.

What felt like ten courses later, there was nothing left on the table and the wine was flowing. The music had kicked in and the Irish in the room were back in default wedding mode. The drink was free and the ceol deafening. What more would you be wanting 10,000 miles from home? In typical Irish fashion, the drink was soon gone. Quite the achievement, if you'd seen the amount there was to get through. The rest of the night is a bit of a blur, but the last thing I remember is playing pool in the Demon bar downtown after leaving the ceremony as part of the stumbling entourage. I knew I needed to get the head together, though. I'd stuff to see in the morning. Hong Kong and the gambling island of Macau were next up on the agenda. By God, I'd miss Shenzhen, though.

5

ISLAND HOPPING

TUESDAY, 2 OCTOBER 2007 – MACAU/HONG KONG

The city of Shenzhen might well be right beside Hong Kong, but there was another point of interest in the vicinity that I hadn't taken into consideration. One of the girls from the GAA club, Emer Carty from Wexford, had taken a few days off after the wedding and she'd agreed to show me the sights of Hong Kong. First, though, we headed to the gambling Mecca of Asia – the Special Administrative Region of Macau. It was a very short hop to Macau from the Chinese mainland, so we headed down to the ferry terminal in Shenzhen. There was minimal customs to go through and, after a comfortable 40-minute ferry ride, we landed in the former Portuguese colony (it was handed back to the Chinese in 1999). The place is incredible, if a little soulless. The first thing that greets you there is an array of massive casinos. Macau grosses more each calendar year than Las Vegas does. The Chinese – or a significant number of them, at least – love to gamble.

While Dalian is one of the most popular holiday destinations for the people of the north around Beijing, Macau is one of the biggest attractions in the south. It's known as the Monte Carlo of the Orient, or East Las Vegas in some parts, and it certainly lives up to its billing – although it is perhaps somewhat less showy than its American cousin.

Gambling has been legal there since the 1850s, when the Portuguese colonialists decided to formalise it. There used to be only Chinese gambling games allowed, but since the introduction of Western gambling machines the place has really taken off. Not unlike the highly detrimental effect the pokie machines have had on the lives of many hapless working-class Australians, it's not long before you see the curse that such gambling establishments can bring. The locals seemed to take little part in the gambling side of things, but I could only imagine how many visiting shirts have been lost here.

It had been great for the economy of Macau, though. The Western gambling corporations had already seen fit to step in for a piece of the lucrative market. There are 28 casinos there already, and several more on the way. The biggest of those, the Venetian, dominates the city's landscape. Emer and I took a nose around the different places, but there wasn't much there for impoverished travelling journalists to get a handle on. The minimum bet was about €20 on the blackjack tables in every casino, so we decided to take a look at the other side of the city instead. But unless you've got heavy pockets, it turns out, there really isn't much else to see.

More importantly, though – there's no GAA club. Time to head on to Hong Kong, I reckoned.

* * *

The rain was teeming from the heavens and nightfall was descending upon the city as we landed on Hong Kong Island. It was the perfect time to see the place for the first time. The massive bay is surrounded by monstrous buildings that dwarf the little ferry on which we were travelling. The city's lights were beginning to come on and it really was a glorious sight. Off the ferry and through customs once more (like Macau, Hong Kong is a Special Administrative Region and maintains its own legal system, police force, monetary system, customs and immigration policies), we headed towards the centre of the city. I had a strong feeling I could well be stuck for a place to stay. Of course, Murphy's Law (I always blame him for my own organisational shortcomings), there was a massive festival on in town and there was no room at any of the inns. Time was beginning to tick on as we got to the tenth booked-up hostel in the city centre area known as Causeway Bay. Thankfully, there was a room there. I dumped the bag, and myself and Emer headed for the pub. Around ten hours earlier I had sworn I'd never drink again. Now, I was just glad to have a roof over my head.

The main strip on Hong Kong Island (which sits opposite the mainland part of the city known as Kowloon) has an excellent subway system linking all the main areas. Causeway Bay and Central sit at either end of a main busy stretch of road and we headed for a bar in the middle of the two – Delaney's in Wanchai.

Hong Kong is one of the easiest cities in Asia to get a feel for straight away, so it's hard to get lost there. Well, proper lost anyway. Delaney's is a nice little bar away from the strains of the bustling city outside. It first opened its doors in 1994 and claims to be the first Irish bar in Hong Kong. A second Delaney's opened within a year on the mainland in Kowloon, and a few years later the group began The Dublin Jack. If not of the first Irish bar in Hong Kong, the group have certainly taken the mantle of the most successful. They also sponsor the Hong Kong GAA club.

After a few beers, weariness got the best of us. It was only a short hop back to Shenzhen for Emer, and I headed for the hotel. Luckily, there was a phone in the room and I set about getting a hold of the GAA lads. I'd only got two days there before I was due to fly to Vietnam, but luckily I got hold of the chairman. Luckier still, he was free for a pint and a chat the next evening.

WEDNESDAY, 3 OCTOBER 2007

A quick exploration of Hong Kong is a real eye-opener. The public transport system is amazing and the shopping is incredible. It's really more like New York, in many ways, than it is like an Asian metropolis. The only real difference is that the Big Apple doesn't have its own Disneyland.

After a long day exploring, I headed to meet up with the president of the local GAA at Dublin Jack's. Fergal Power was sitting upstairs at the bar as I walked in. It's a nice bar, quite reminiscent of a pub in Ireland, but much smokier. The smoking ban hasn't hit there yet, and ashtrays and matchboxes line the counter. Thirsty as be damned, I pulled up a chair at the bar alongside Fergal. The storied history of Hong Kong GAA is, unfortunately, far too long to fit in this book. Power, however, ran me through some of the highlights of his tenure at the helm.

Originally from Whitehall in north Dublin, Power was never really involved in his local GAA club at home – Whitehall Colmcilles; he was always more of a soccer man. However, when he came to Hong Kong with work all that changed. He soon realised what he'd been missing out on all those years and wasn't long in swelling the ranks of the city's GAA, eventually rising to a position of great influence. He was seeking to build a new life in a far-away city, and although never having been what you might call a GAA diehard in Dublin, when in a strange and foreign land people tend to gravitate towards what they know.

There have been some serious highlights in recent years at the club, but the biggest was almost certainly the All Stars tour of 2005 (where the best Gaelic footballers of 2004 took on the best of the current year in an exhibition clash).

The club there is huge, alongside Singapore and Dubai in stature, even perhaps dwarfing both of those. I reckoned it was the biggest club in Asia. Many famous faces had come through there over the years; in fact, former Laois star M.J. Tierney would be player of the tournament in Hong Kong's colours the following year at the Asian Games in Malaysia. Many more like him are sure to do likewise in the not too distant future.

Power has fond memories of that 2005 All Stars tour. The tourists had brought along the award-winning footballers of 2003 and 2004, and greats such as Peter Canavan, Declan Browne and Padraig Joyce were all on board. So was then Taoiseach Bertie Ahern and that darling of Asian GAA, former association president Seán Kelly. An individual spoken more highly of I reckon I'd struggle to find in any circle. Outside of the impressive guest list, though, it was the organisation of the whole event that pleased Power as much as anything. It was widely regarded as one of the best All Stars tours in history. Journalists and officials raved about it at the time. From top-notch hotels and footballing facilities to a booze cruise that will live long in the memory of many of those who attended, it was something to be proud of. Power certainly still was.

Hong Kong had built from that event, but the foundations for a successful GAA club were already there. Although more than 2,000 people attended the All Stars game, the expat population in the city has always been strong. The summer leagues offer a great insight into the scope and scale of the GAA operation. The club utilise five different grounds on and off – Aberdeen, King George V, Happy Valley, King's Park and the Hong Kong Football Club, which hosted the All Stars game itself. There are also eight club teams here that compete in the summer leagues. In men's football, Kowloon Kickhams, Shek O O'Tooles, Wan Chai St Kevin's and Lumma Fr Murphy's line out, while Admiralty Crokes, North Point Na Fianna, Stanley Setanta and Chai Wan Colmcilles all play in the ladies' football league. The GAA there is an institution for Irish expats. No better way to find your feet in a strange and foreign land.

A fact not too well known is that Hong Kong and Ireland also have a mutual working holiday visa agreement. This allows 100 Irish travellers per year to call the city home (and vice versa Hong Kong visitors in Ireland). The biggest attraction to the city seems to be the regular and stable employment opportunities for the highly skilled. If you're a banker or a fund accountant for a major firm, for example, it's quite likely your company will have an office here. So many Irish expats call Hong Kong home, for a few years at least, and the GAA club grows in strength from the arrival and involvement of each and every one.

Hong Kong is still a part of China despite an array of trimmings that could easily lead the visitor to believe otherwise. The club there normally play in the All-China Games (and more often than not win it). That year, though, they had given Dalian a miss. Hong Kong, you see, were back in Ireland at the Kilmacud Crokes Sevens at the time. The standard of football is exceptionally high and proof of that fact could be seen by how just how well the team had performed at that event in Dublin. It's not a cheap exercise heading to Ireland en masse, especially having already been in Singapore for the Asian Games and in Dubai for the Gulf Games earlier that year. They weren't just going to Dublin for show, though. And it wasn't made easy for them, as they were drawn in a tough group with Bryansford from Down, Antrim's Cregan Kickhams and Galway's Tuam Stars. Hong Kong, rather incredibly in many people's minds, beat three-times Crokes Sevens champions Bryansford in their first game. They lost the rest of their games, but you get the point. They're no mugs.

The club has been going here since 1995 and its foundation coincided with the construction of Hong Kong International Airport. A large number of Irish architects and engineers descended upon the city and, as is the case with so many cities around the world, a GAA club soon followed.

From Dublin Jack's, Fergal took me on a little bar crawl around the city. Delaney's, of course, was involved, as were about three other bars. It's a great city by night and really rivals New York in the 'city that never sleeps' stakes. I, on the other hand, do sleep. I had a flight to Hanoi early in the morning. Hong Kong, I promised myself as I hit the bed for the night, will someday be revisited. I'd only scratched the surface.

6

THE VIET CELTS

It was warm and balmy as I landed in Hanoi. It was still monsoon season there and you could almost taste the moisture on the air. The journey had been relatively simple, though. The trip to the airport in Hong Kong was short and sweet, just a hop and a jump onto a train and within 20 minutes I was sitting in the airport scoffing down a Burger King. It's a pretty busy airport, but there's an element of organised chaos that offers the weary traveller some home comforts. It's as modern as you're likely to find anywhere in the world. A far cry from what I would discover in Vietnam.

From Hanoi airport, I grabbed a cab to the city centre. The roads from the airport were not what you might call highways and I was nervous as the car bounced along the scraggly track and into the city. The buildings that flank the main road into Hanoi are run-down and the place looks dirty. The streets are lined with smiling happy faces, though, and if the buildings that surround betray the cruelty of poverty, the expressions and manner of the local people do anything but. The place was thronged to the gills with mopeds racing about their daily business. We turned off down a side alleyway and I paid the taxi man with my newly acquired Vietnamese dong before grabbing my bags and heading for my new temporary home.

The hostel was right in the middle of the city and run by one of the most jovial Aussies you're likely to come across. I'd been told about this place by a fellow traveller in Beijing and was assured that the craic would be mighty and the bags safe. There's not much more you can ask for. I was standing in the queue behind two typically well-organised but slightly befuddled Germans when I spotted an advert on the noticeboard. The rest of the postings were hand-written and scrawled on copybook paper, but this one had the look of a professionally done job behind it. 'Looking for a great way to meet friends and stay fit in Hanoi?' it read. 'Then come join the Hanoi Swans footie team. Training every Wednesday night, bus leaves the hostel at 7.30 p.m.' Recruiting for the local Aussie Rules team in the hostel? I was going to like this place.

With my bags safely stowed away under the bed, I grabbed a map and set about having a quick look around the city before darkness got its grubby hands on it. Out the door and down the laneway, I was quickly taken aback (literally) by the hordes of mopeds that were still flowing through the city's streets. The place was crazy.

I knew there wasn't much time to look around before nightfall, and I also didn't want to be too far from a friendly face when the light tucked itself away for the evening. It's not that I'm afraid of the dark, it's just that on first impressions the place was rough. The average Vietnamese, by the looks of things anyway, barely had two pennies to rub together.

I wandered around a few corners and into a main crossroads, which scared the living daylights out of me. There was no such thing as traffic lights or green men. Close your eyes, run, and hope for the best seemed to be the local way of getting to the other side of the street. Luckily, my experiences in Beijing had taught me a few nifty tricks. Make sure you've got a local on either side of you as you're crossing the road. They seem to know what they're doing.

Two or three blocks were enough for me. I was tired and an angry cloud was darkening the sky even further. I found my way back to the hostel quickly enough and retired to the porch with a beer in hand. Safe. The humidity was frightening and you just knew there was a storm coming. The heavens duly opened as an Aussie to my left opened up a conversation.

Todd Clarke had been in Hanoi for a few weeks and loved it. Working on an ocean research vessel for his day job, he'd seen a lot of things in his relatively short twenty-nine years and after eight months at sea he'd decided to spend his few months off in South East Asia. He'd seen neighbouring Cambodia and Laos, and was considering staying on in Hanoi for a few months. The ad for the local footie team seemed to have sealed the deal for him in that regard. A few beers later and one of the owners had sat down to join us for a beer.

'Aussie' Mick had started the place back in December 2004 with his mate Max and converted it from a former diplomat's house into what he tells us is Hanoi's first and only international backpacker's hostel. He hands me another beer as he tells us this, so I wasn't going to argue. The buildings there are all very narrow and close together, and Mick tells us that it's from when the French were there. The former colonists used to charge by area for the land and so everyone had decided to build up instead of out. Another theory is to do with the sheer volume of rain that falls here during the monsoon season. It was seriously bucketing outside, so both arguments carried weight.

The mosquitoes had decided to join us at that stage, too, so I decided to call it a night. There was nowhere to be going in that rain, anyway.

FRIDAY, 5 OCTOBER 2007

A beam of golden sunlight cut through the room as I opened my eyes in the cramped and crowded 12-bed dorm. The rain had come and gone, but as I stared out from the balcony at the puddles on the streets you could see it hadn't been gone for long. I reacquainted myself with the map and set about making a plan of action for the day ahead. I was about six blocks from the hostel when I discovered something more startling than my last-minute glimpse of the twelve or so mopeds that had attempted to run me down en route. Beside an inner-city park that also housed a local museum sat the most unlikely of signs: a big glistening 'KFC'. I had been told that there were no McDonald's in the entire country and so had assumed that this applied to all the fast-food chains. The boys from Kentucky seemed to have found their way in. And from what I could see, business was booming. After a curious look around at the clientele, I continued off on my way. I hadn't seen a bus yet, and taxis seemed to operate solely out of the airport, from what I could tell. I hadn't been able to find a single thing I had been searching for and I soon realised that the KFC was the only landmark I recognised since I'd left the hostel two hours previously. Unfortunately, KFC wasn't even on the map. I knew I was completely lost. The only thing I could see was a large railway station. A massive train had just pulled in, pretty much straight off the street into a shed-like structure. Desperately searching for white faces anywhere, and in need of a nudge in the right direction, I started getting paranoid and was beginning to feel pairs of eyes training on my increasingly perilous situation. I was furiously hoping they couldn't smell the fear.

Everything looked the same and I couldn't read any of the signs. I was trying to match the street names on my map with any available road signs, but I wasn't having a huge amount of luck. I eventually found myself back in the relative solace of KFC, and sat down to gather myself. It wasn't a city I fancied getting lost in. Clearly seeing the signs of distress on my furrowed brow, a nice American couple approached and pointed me in the right direction . . . The only place I thought I'd need to get directions from an American was in America.

I was feeling pretty useless by this point. Tired, sweaty and slightly embarrassed, I found the hostel with my tail between my legs and settled down with Mick, who'd perched himself in the doorway once again. I told him my tale of woe in the hope that he might have a helpful hint to avoid a similar disaster on my next voyage. The one tip he did give me proved the best I could have hoped for: hold the map the right way up. It seems my directional base had been upside down, as the hostel was marked on the wrong side of the alleyway on the map. Todd wandered down while I was still a crimson shade of red. He suggested we grab a beer. Best idea I'd heard all day. Luckily, he knew a place. And the best way to get there.

We wandered to the top of the alleyway and Todd stuck out his hand into the main roadway. I wasn't sure what he was expecting to happen. All I could see were millions of mopeds swarming in either direction. Within thirty seconds, two had pulled in alongside us and Todd had climbed on the back of the first one, while encouraging me to do the same on the second. I was slightly nervous. These guys were homicidal, suicidal, off-the-bridle maniacs around these little streets, and I was bricking it. I didn't know where we were going, but it was certainly better than wandering the streets alone with an upside down map and a big 'sucker' sign plastered on my forehead.

'Follow that guy,' I mumbled, pointing to the moped in front, and like a flash we were zooming non-stop through busy crossroads at what felt like 100 mph. With gums for earrings, I peeled myself off the bike at an inauspicious-looking street corner, handed the driver a 20,000-dong note (about one euro) and followed Todd's gestures. My eyes followed his pointing finger to the sign above his head: Finnegan's Irish bar. Ah, where would you be . . .

I wasn't sure just quite what to expect as I rolled on in through the door. Todd seemed to know the guys behind the counter, so I cosied up and ordered a beer. There was one white guy and a Vietnamese girl serving and two other white guys perched at either end of the bar. It's a small world here if you're a white guy and the clientele were keen to chat to any new arrival. The barman and the guy at the far end were in their mid-20s and we soon got to chatting. Turns out they were from Kildare and both worked there at the bar. A friend of theirs had come out here on a holiday a few years back and had ended up buying a part of the little bar. They were now out there teaching English and doing some bar work on the side. The Vietnamese girl owned the other half, it transpired, and the two lads weren't long telling me about their lives in Hanoi. Quiet, simple, rewarding work and, most important of all, the cost of living is next to nothing. It sure does sound tempting, I told them, but they were out to prove their point.

Seven hours and a mighty skinful of porter later, I found myself on the back of one of their mopeds heading down the deserted streets towards the Red River. It was pitch black and the only sound was the music pumping out of the local nightclub we were about to enter. The bouncers had long gone home and the only people in the club were the bar staff, who had remained behind for a few late drinks. After three or four more drinks, and at a total cost of around two euros, I wandered out the back to the balcony that overlooked the river. The nightclub itself was reminiscent of an old abandoned castle you might have drunk cans in as a teenager in Dublin in the early '90s. The balcony at the back looked like something the council at home would surely have either knocked down or cordoned off some years before. But the view of the rising sun across the river was enough to take me away from the unstable surroundings. One of the lads joined me and explained that the only real danger was the swarms of rats that wandered up from the riverbanks. That was enough for me. After a mountain of gargle and a 20-minute hell-for-leather moped journey home, I was certainly glad to see my *leaba*. The sun had already risen as I rocked back into the hostel, and the Germans had gathered in the lobby ready for day trips around the city and beyond. I was fit for bed, and was soon in it, having nightmares about giant rats and crazy moped drivers.

SATURDAY, 6 OCTOBER 2007

The sound of what I reckoned had to be a beating drum stirred me from my coma. My head felt rough, to say the least, and my groggy eyes were looking around, trying to find the source of all the noise. All the other beds in the room were empty and the curtains were slightly open to reveal a star-filled sky. A quick check of the watch told me it was 6.30 p.m. I stepped across to answer the door that had been thumping for the last five minutes. Todd was standing there, bright as a button, with a big smile on his face, a beer in his hand and a Wallabies jersey straddled proudly about his shoulders. I quickly threw on some clothes and followed him up to the rooftop bar for 'breakfast'. Or, more accurately, the beers and barbecue they hold there at the hostel every night.

I reached the rooftop, where Todd introduced me to his new mate, a burly Kiwi named Dan. He was about 30 and all togged out in his All Blacks gear. I looked around and soon spotted that Aussie Mick also had his native green-and-gold on board. With all the travelling and the heavy night before, I'd completely lost track of time. And of the rugby. The Aussies were set to take on England in a few hours' time and Todd had felt certain he'd recruited a worthy ally in the boozy Irish guy from the hostel. He wasn't too sure which side of the fence Dan might fall on. Either way, two burgers and a few beers later we were en route back down to Finnegan's.

All was surreally quiet as we walked in the doorway. The tired faces of my new Kildare mates were there to greet us, though. One was on the cure, the other on the job behind the bar. Heavy going. We settled into one of the booths as the commentators prepared us for the match ahead. It was the South African sports channel again, so they were naturally shouting for the Aussies. They were also making very little effort to hide that fact in their pre-match build-up. There were two English guys in the bar and they weren't shy in pumping out a rousing version of 'God Save the Queen' before Todd, and a small handful of his countrymen, answered in kind with 'Advance Australia Fair'. We decided to make a little wager between the three of us. In the interests of being awkward, and as part of some newly discovered affection for my fellow man from the northern hemisphere, I took England and France to beat the Aussies and the Kiwis respectively. It was only 100,000 dong or so. Turned out to be great value for money.

I was sure Todd's face had gone through the full range of human emotions by the time the final whistle sounded on his country's shock 12–10 defeat. The English fans in the bar were, of course, gracious as ever in victory. It was only when I suggested that a round of beers might suffice as payment instead of the 100,000 dong I'd wagered that real darkness fell upon his face and the excuses began pouring from his lips. Australia, he explained, had wanted to lose that game. A clearout was needed of all the old guard. George Gregan, Stephen Larkham and those guys had run their course in the national colours and change was badly needed. Fresh blood. A smile began to creep across my face.

Dan, of course, was grinning from ear to ear. His happy demeanour, just like all Kiwis when the All Blacks are playing, had changed to one of sheer focus and determination as New Zealand took the field for their quarter-final against France. His eyes had barely left the beer Todd had reluctantly bought him in payment for his losing bet as the anthems rang out. My Aussie mate, on the other hand, was barely choking his down in disgust. I wondered if he'd ever smile again. Eighty minutes' worth of rugby later, I had my answer. France 20, New Zealand 18. Ouch.

A moped ride, two rugby matches and ten beers in Hanoi: 200,000 dong. Two arrogant southern hemisphere rugby fans that had just been stuffed by two 'weaker' teams from the north: priceless.

SUNDAY, 7 OCTOBER 2007

Sunday morning arrived and I headed down to the lobby of the hostel to check my emails. I had sent Seán Hoy a message a few weeks previously about catching up with him in Hanoi for a chat about the local GAA club there, the Viet Celts. Local is probably a poor choice of word, though. The Celts are the only club in the country and Hoy had founded them just a year earlier ahead of the Asian Games in Singapore. Working for the Irish Foreign Service over the years had taken him to all sorts of exotic places, but it was in Vietnam that he had set up his first and only GAA club. A Fermanagh native, Hoy had actually set up the first Irish Embassy in Vietnam and was based in Hanoi in his role as head of development for the Embassy of Ireland. Luckily, he was free that evening, so we decided to meet up in Finnegan's. As good a place as any.

I headed down early to prepare a few questions with what limited information I had on the club and was sitting in the booth nearest the door as Seán walked in with his motorbike helmet under his arm. It seemed to be the best way to get around, even for the Westerners. He had travelled in from his home outside the city and sat down just as the Fiji versus South Africa game came on the screen. There seemed to be a bigger crowd than there had been the night before, for some reason.

After some gentle prodding, Seán started to tell me about the little GAA club he'd established there in Vietnam.

It had all begun the year before, when he had gathered a group of guys together for the Asian Games in Singapore. With support from a few local companies such as Finnegan's, Tiger Air and the only other Irish bar in Vietnam, Sheridan's in Ho Chi Minh City, they had put together a team and headed for Singapore, which is only a short hop to the south. They might not have set the tournament alight with their football skills, but their antics had become the stuff of legend in Asia. The lads in China and Dubai weren't able to tell me too much about the Viet Celts, or any of their players, or even mentors Seán, Colm Ross or Steve Kinlough in Ho Chi Minh, but the one thing they did remember was that the Celts had presented every team they played with a bottle of Vietnamese vodka before each game. It's the little things that sometimes matter most.

The club was only in its infancy, but there was great hope for the future. Like most Asian GAA clubs, with the exception of maybe Japan, Singapore and Hong Kong, expats from other nations are key to keeping the club populated and moving forward. The Celts already had a few English, Aussies, Americans and French on board in that regard. Indeed, Seán had already had success within the local population, recruiting a local lad to travel with the team to Singapore for the Asian Games. The Viet Celts are distinct in one way in that the club is split into two main centres: Hanoi, the capital, to the far north, and Ho Chi Minh City, or Saigon, as it's also known, in the far south. The club's membership is split between the two, with a few other players scattered in places such as Hue on the central coast. The main ethos is to have some fun and they only really gather once or twice a year to travel to play in tournaments.

The ability to host their own annual event and to welcome teams from other countries to Vietnam would also prove key. By June of the following year, Seán would have achieved that goal, as the Celts hosted their first tournament in Ciputra International City in Hanoi. Teams from Singapore and Malaysia would come to take on the Vietnamese lads, as Singapore won both the men's and women's tournaments. The Celts, however, would do exceedingly well to come second in both. Baby steps.

The following year the club would travel to Penang in Malaysia for the Asian Games, but for now the building blocks had been put in place and strong links with neighbouring clubs in Bangkok, Singapore and Malaysia would ultimately provide a sufficiently competitive calendar of events to keep the newly converted GAA folk interested. There might not have been a McDonald's, but there were now at least as many GAA clubs in Vietnam as there were KFCs. Now that's a sentence I never thought I'd be writing this time three years ago, when there wasn't even an Irish Embassy there.

I left Seán there as he headed for home, but I'd got all I needed. There was no 120-year history of GAA in Hanoi (yet), and a simple grounding in how they came about and what made them tick was all I really needed. Also, some travel tips. Seán recommended that I headed to a place called Halong Bay on the north-east coast for a few days. Some non-GAA related activities sounded appealing, so I headed back to the hostel and booked the three-day trip, which included an overnight cruise. Without wanting to sound too much like the Vietnamese tourist board, if you're ever in Vietnam make sure you go to Halong Bay. It takes four hours on a minibus to get there from Hanoi, but think nineteenth-century villages with mopeds. At one point I even spotted a pair of the two-wheeled demons overtaking our bus with a couple of giant 20-stone pigs tied to the back upside down and very much alive, with their tongues hanging out. The only thing more surreal was the Vengaboys cassette our bus driver insisted on playing non-stop the entire way there and back.

After two days at sea, meandering through the thousands of uninhabited islands that jut out of the sea while feasting on local wild fruits and chilling with sunset dips in the ocean, it was time to move on to my second-last stop in Asia. A farther cry from the peace of Halong Bay there could surely not have been. Onwards to Bangkok.

7

THAI GAAs AND THE ORANG ÉIRE

THURSDAY, 11 OCTOBER 2007 – BANGKOK

After three long weeks and more than 10,000 miles of travelling solo, I arrived in Bangkok to meet three friends – Ger Power, Mark Moran and Joey Cassidy – from my hometown of Lucan. I was looking forward to seeing some familiar faces, and luckily they'd landed in the Thai capital without a hitch. That was about as far as our organisational skills had taken any of us, though, and so we set about making a plan for the night ahead. My Kiwi friend in Hanoi had just come from Bangkok and he'd recommended a good place to stay in the city away from all the backpacker hustle and bustle. The plan was soon set and the four of us headed for the taxi rank.

After 25 minutes or so in a cab, we pulled up on Sukhumvit soi 25. The streets in Bangkok are called sois and in a way it makes life pretty easy when it comes to getting around. The lads were excited, having hopefully left the wet and windy winter of the Emerald Isle behind, and we checked into our hostel, which was more like a five-star hotel compared to what I'd experienced thus far in Asia. The weather had been abysmal in Ireland for the past three weeks, the lads tell me, as we sit down for a pizza dinner in the first restaurant we see. Then, on cue, the skies opened up to unleash the worst rainstorm any of us had ever seen. God bless them, their faces dropped. We decided to stay in for the night with a bottle of whiskey and a deck of cards.

FRIDAY, 12 OCTOBER 2007

Sunny skies were there to greet us the following morning, as we met for breakfast downstairs outside the hostel. We had four different maps out on the table, as we set about making our way around the massive city. Bangkok is renowned for its shopping malls and in particular the world famous BKM Center, or Mahboonkrong, as it's also known. The lads wanted to buy cameras and get some cheap clothes, and there is no better place than the enormous marble shopping mall. At eight storeys high, and 330 metres long, with 2,500 shops, it certainly knocks the Square in Tallaght flat on its backside.

The public transportation system is safe, cheap and simple, and although we were still all right for cash we avoided the taxi route and headed for the famous Skytrain. After a few hours' shopping, we came away happy with our purchases and headed for the hostel to prepare for the night ahead. We'd obviously heard a lot about the seedy nature of the city we were visiting, but the previous night's explorations hadn't taken us too far from the hostel, so we had no idea just how close to the middle of all that action we really were.

After a few drinks in the room, we headed off around the corner to where we could hear music and what sounded like a massive street party in full swing. It was only 9 p.m. or so, but the place was kicking. Then, before our eyes, we saw the infamous Soi Cowboy lit up like a dingy version of the Vegas Strip.

Soi Cowboy basically rose around the US Army when they were stationed there during the Vietnam War. It has pretty much retained that same 'charm' ever since. It was definitely not our cup of tea, but we put our heads down and embarked off down the main promenade for a look around. Within five minutes, hordes of scantily clad girls were hanging off our arms and repeating the phrase 'handsome man' over and over again, trying to drag us into whichever of the hundred or so 'bars' along the street they happened to be working for. We were halfway up when it all started to get a bit much. It was too late to turn back at that stage, though, so we braved our way to the end of the 200-metre-long street. We thought we'd seen it all when a random elephant and a man holding a bag of fruit came waltzing by nonchalantly. Calm as you like, normal as a cup of tea in the morning. This really was a strange, strange place.

Thirsty for respite and shelter from the hordes of mad women who seemed to be following us with disappointed bleats of broken English, we spotted a sign for a sports bar at the end of the street. Sanctuary. Within minutes, we were snug in the Down Under bar, tucking into a few local beers. Once again the Aussies had come through for me and we sat satisfied as we looked wearily back out the window at the madness. We weren't heading out of that bar any time soon, we thought to ourselves. Turned out it would actually take us a week or so to leave the place.

SATURDAY, 13 OCTOBER 2007

It was pitch black outside when we woke up after our first night out in Bangkok. We had no idea what time it was, but could hear the music pounding out from across the street once again and could only assume it was night-time. We couldn't remember much about the night before, other than the fact that we'd left the Down Under bar when it was bright with the promise that we'd return for the World Cup semi-final that night. We assumed it was about time for kick-off in the France v. England game, so shook off the cobwebs and headed down to the bar.

In pure Aussie style, all the beers were served in padded sleeves to keep them cold. Stubby-holders, as they're known in Oz. There was no real need for them in Thailand at that time of year, but the sentiment remained. Something on the sleeve of my beer soon caught my eye, intriguing me. It seemed the All-Asian AFL Championships had been held there a few months previously and the Down Under had been one of the main sponsors. Teams from all over Asia, including some brilliantly named sides such as the Bali Geckos, the Hong Kong Dragons, the Jakarta Bingtangs, the Lao Elephants, the Malaysian Warriors, the Tokyo Goannas and the Singapore Wombats, had come to compete alongside the Swans from Hanoi, the Dingoes from Dubai and the local team, the Thailand Tigers. It also turned out that Mick, the guy that ran the bar there, knew Aussie Mick from the hostel in Hanoi. Small world. I was beginning to wonder just how much more the Aussie Rules boys had in common with the GAA.

The bar had been fairly quiet when we'd landed. As it turned out we were actually well early for kick-off. But as I looked around from beer number five, I noticed that the place had suddenly filled with English jerseys. Mick seemed glad to have us there for company. Sadly, our presence could do very little to stop the rampaging Pommies beating the host nation 14–9. Chorus after chorus of 'Swing Low, Sweet Chariot' began wafting through the air, along with a sense of dread for the upcoming final the following Sunday. Lord save us if they won it, they'd be simply unbearable.

There was talk from the loud English group in the corner of calling the Down Under bar home for the week until the final the following weekend. We looked up and exchanged glances with one another, and with Mick, who was clearly filled with a mixture of dread at the thought of having to entertain a gaggle of obnoxious English fans and the amount of money he was surely going to make from the exercise. You got the impression he wasn't there to make money, though. He had about six female bar staff on duty every night. The number of patrons in there would rarely exceed ten on a weekend.

We decided to hang around the city until the final and have a decent look around in the meantime. Of course, we'd have darkened the door of the Down Under bar several times by the following weekend. Far from the madding crowd.

THAI GAAs AND THE ORANG ÉIRE

By Friday afternoon, I'd heard back from Derry native John Campbell of the local GAA club in Bangkok. The rather brilliantly christened Thai GAAs were having a pre-season get-together that night in the Dubliner bar and he'd invited me to come along. I was looking at the directions and Skytrain timetable he'd emailed when I realised that the bar was literally across the other side of the motorway from where we were staying. Incredibly, we hadn't come across it in our eight days in the city. Joey, Mark and Ger decided to tag along, as we headed across just after sunset and landed to find a boisterous crowd in full voice as county colours swarmed the upstairs and downstairs of the bar. A man in a Tyrone jersey was belting out ballads from the stage.

It wasn't unlike any other Irish bar around the world, but it still seemed odd that there were quite so many Irish people in such a place. We wondered where they'd all been hiding. I eventually tracked down John Campbell, who was sitting downstairs with his wife as I approached for a chat. He was in great form and told how the club had really turned their fortunes around in recent times. Apparently, there had been a GAA club there a number of years back, but it had fallen apart sometime before. Since then, he and a few colleagues had been busy rebuilding. Judging by the energetic crowd on hand, things were going well in that regard.

John and I had been chatting for about ten minutes when he introduced me to a young man in his 20s. Eoin Duggan was the first secretary at the Irish Embassy in Kuala Lumpur and he'd just started the first GAA club in Malaysia. Chance encounter. Lovely. The Orang Éire club had been founded earlier that year, Eoin told me. The word 'Orang', he said, comes from Bahasa Malay and means 'people'. As seemed to be the continuing trend, Orang Éire had members from Australia and New Zealand, but rather interestingly they also had players from even more unlikely places, such as Hungary and South Africa. Hey, the more the merrier.

Just like the Viet Celts, Orang Éire had been founded ahead of the Asian Games the previous June and from there they had begun to grow. Eoin was soon excitedly explaining the club's plans to start an underage training scheme early the following year and that the club's first tournament was set to be held a few weeks later in Malaysia.

The KL Challenge Cup would see teams from Singapore and Thailand head south in November. In what seemed to be the norm, teams in such secluded regions really depended on their own tournaments and their neighbours' events to keep things going. The Thai GAAs were preparing to host the first-ever Thailand Invitational Tournament in April 2008, with Malaysia, Hong Kong and Singapore all set to visit. It really was important to capitalise on such early successes. Orang would also travel to Hanoi for the Celts' tournament the following June. Orang Éire's success looked guaranteed going forward, but another young club would also pop up in Malaysia ahead of the 2008 Asian Games. The Penang Pumas, from the host city, were only at the embryonic stage of their development, but the close ties between the university there and University College Dublin (UCD) and the Royal College of Surgeons in Ireland meant that there were steady streams of young Malaysian students heading to Ireland and vice versa. Surely a recipe for more success in the future. Indeed, Mícheál Ó Muircheartaigh would make his way to Penang en route to the International Rules series in Australia in October 2008.

Ultan Peters had been one of the main guys behind the formation of the original Bangkok club back in 2004, alongside John Murray and with help from Singapore's Peter Ryan and Hong Kong's Fergal Power. The Bangkok team had travelled to Hong Kong that year for the Asian Games, but it took another three years before a team from Thailand would return to the Games in Singapore in 2007. Campbell, Derek Martin and Peters eventually got the show up and running again and they seemed on the road to securing a prosperous future. I left John safe in the knowledge that all was well on the whole for the GAA in South East Asia. I was sure I'd learn more when I reached Singapore in a few weeks' time to meet up with the chairman and secretary of the Asian County Board.

The following evening we honoured our word and headed back to the Down Under bar for the Rugby World Cup final. Our English pals seemed to have doubled in number in the week that had passed in between, but they were soon sitting quietly in the corner as the Springboks, who had climbed out from amongst the Bangkok woodwork, sprung into full voice. We wondered if the English lads were planning to hang around for another week now. And thought not. Either way, we were out of there on a holiday through the islands of Thailand and the temples of Cambodia for a few weeks. Tough work, but someone's got to do it.

FRIDAY, 9 NOVEMBER 2007 – BANGKOK

My last act in Bangkok before heading south had been to store my laptop and all the notes and interview tapes I had gathered over my travels through the Gulf and Asia safely in the hostel. I had been assured the storage location was a secure room and so I also decided to throw most of my bank cards, flight tickets and travellers cheques in there while I was at it. A credit card, passport and a bag of clothes, I thought, would do the trick for a few weeks after a month of lugging baggage around with me. After a heavy few weeks of travelling through dirt tracks and decrepit accommodations, I was glad I'd done it. I had no doubt the stuff would have gone missing while I was either pulling it through the jungles of Cambodia or island hopping in southern Thailand. But it seemed I was doomed, no matter what I did.

I had arrived back in Bangkok the night before from Ho Chi Minh City in south Vietnam, where I had popped in to visit Steve Kinlough, the man who looked after the southern half of the Viet Celts. A former top-class soccer player in his day, he had taken time out from his work as a travel agent to tell me a little more about the club and to show me around. We had been in Ho Chi Minh for a few days and had seen the famous Cu Chi tunnels and all the rest, but the monsoon rain had failed to leave our side for long. The three lads had headed on north into Laos to try the famous tubing down the Vang Vieng River, but I had made my way back to Bangkok for a connecting flight to Singapore the following day. A good night's sleep in a proper bed had me fully refreshed and eager to get on with things as I approached the hostel desk that morning to settle the bill. All smiles, no worries; there seemed to be a queue of taxis waiting outside, so I feared little for my prospects of making the airport in time for my flight to Singapore, even though it was set to depart in two hours' time. Just the small matter of retrieving all my worldly possessions.

About 15 minutes had passed as the young guy behind the counter scrambled around with an increasingly concerned look on his face. My brow, also increasingly burdened with concern, was becoming somewhat furrowed. Almost half an hour had passed when he nervously approached the counter for a fifth time to enquire as to the shape and colour of the bag in question. Trying to stay calm, I repeated my response. He shook his head and averted his gaze from my glaring eyes. Are you actually kidding me, mate? He apologised and explained that someone else must have come in and taken my bag by mistake. I could feel a certain darkness creep across my face. My flight was by then an hour away and I was full sure I was turning blue. All I had in my possession was one credit card – which was in need of a serious recharge, which I couldn't do without my other bank card in the bag – and my passport. Deep breaths. Money can be replaced. A month's worth of research, notes and interviews from seven Asian and Gulf cities on a once-in-a-lifetime trip, on the other hand, could not. My heart froze as I realised there was nothing I could do. The young man handed me a phone with his boss at the other end, but unfortunately his assurances in broken English that he would find the bag mattered very little to a traveller of no fixed abode, with no forwarding address to send it to even if he did. I knew he was very unlikely to find it, anyway; in fact, it was even more unlikely that he'd even look for it. With a heavy heart and a feeling of complete helplessness, I left my email address, muttered some profanities as Gaeilge and headed for the nearest cab. My head was spinning.

THAI GAAs AND THE ORANG ÉIRE

Some form of festival was blocking the road to the airport from the hostel as we pulled around the corner. My flight was due to leave in less than an hour now and I was at least 30 minutes away from checking in. The only respite had come with the knowledge that the innovation of the e-ticket meant I could just reprint my ticket at the airport, and indeed that my passport would suffice as collateral to get me on the plane. That was all correct and proper, of course. Unfortunately, it doesn't do you much good when you're 20 minutes late for check-in.

Needless to say, I missed the flight. Trying to stay calm, I duly booked another one. Losing the rag wasn't going to help my situation, although I will admit I was on the brink and harboured some seriously vengeful thoughts. My time in Thailand had been wonderful and quite the adventure, and I'd like to think the rage I had at losing so much time and effort might have subsided by now – in reality, though, I still want to strangle the bastards. One stop left in Asia, then it was back to Western society.

Good morning, Singapore.

8

THE HEALING POWERS OF THE GALTEE SAUSAGE

SATURDAY, 10 NOVEMBER 2007 – SINGAPORE

With a big stressball head on me, I had landed safely in Singapore the night before and booked myself a private room in a downtown hotel. A calm night of screaming profanities into my pillow without having 11 strangers throwing funny looks in my direction seemed the least I could do for myself, as I came to terms with my tremendous loss. I only had two days in Singapore before I flew to Sydney, and so I knew I'd have plenty to do to keep my mind off things.

I left the hotel bright and early the next morning for a look around and soon found my way to Muddy Murphy's Irish bar for a consolatory Irish fry-up. Feeling like a new man after scoffing down about 12 slices of brown bread and a pot of tea, I headed for the Western Union to pick up an emergency money transfer from home. Things could certainly have been a lot worse, to be fair – or so I consoled myself. I could rewrite what I'd lost and there was a bank account I'd set up in Australia sitting waiting for me. All I needed was enough to get me through two days in Singapore – the equivalent of what would have lasted me two weeks in Thailand! Unfortunately, Singapore is more like Hong Kong than Phuket, and it turned out that I had barely enough for a few pints and a bit of breakfast. Lesson learned, though. Stuff happens. Gotta get on with it.

I'd been in fairly regular email contact with Paraic McGrath since departing from Dublin and I was looking forward to catching up with him in Singapore. He'd been living here for a few years now and had been operating from the city as chairman of the Asian County Board through his involvement with the Singapore Gaelic Lions GAA club. I got in touch with him after doing my business at the local Western Union and he gave me a few tips for a nice beer and a bit of grub that night. Most cities with large Irish populations tend to have a touristy Irish bar, and then one the local residents actually frequent. In this particular case, it appeared that Molly Malone's was the local hotspot. Located in the busy bar district of Boat Quay, it was a bit of a trek from the hostel by foot, but a taxi had me sitting in front of a creamy Guinness within 15 minutes and I couldn't have been happier. It's amazing how you can go from the lowest ebb to complete contentedness in the space of 24 hours, with the aid of a decent fry-up and a few pints of the black stuff.

With the blood pressure back under control, I set about having a wander around Molly Malone's and soon I discovered a small room out the back of the pub. The discovery, by all accounts, was the Gaelic Lions GAA clubhouse. Jerseys and team pictures adorned the walls and a big screen sat in the corner, where, I learned, the local Gaels gathered to watch the GAA from home every Sunday during the summer. Alone in a pub, almost completely broke and 8,000 miles from home, yet there was something comforting in seeing smiling GAA team photos hanging on the wall.

I slept well that night. The following morning I'd attend the first-ever underage hurling training session in Singapore.

SUNDAY, 11 NOVEMBER 2007

Paraic greeted me with a cheery smile as I climbed into his car on the way to the training field. The club had been running underage football sessions at Turf City for some time now, with the children of expat families of all denominations joining in the fun. After a quick pitstop to pick up his kids, we soon pulled up at the abandoned racetrack and Paraic headed for the boot to take out the few hurls and sliotars he'd gathered together for the session. His excited youngsters leapt from the car and ran towards the pitch and their awaiting friends and teammates. His plan for today was to introduce the kids to the small ball as part of a sort of 'slowly but surely' process. The first half of the session would be football, as per usual, but then the older group would get to puc around for the first time together. Paraic had been promising to let the kids play some hurling for months. They'd been chomping at the bit, he tells me. They barely even want to bother with the football.

The Go-Games mini goalposts were quickly set up, as the children were divided into groups by age. Paraic took the older group over to a separate field, while the other trainers, a hardy group of volunteers, took two other groups onto the main field. After a series of kicking drills, a game broke out and it was like something you'd expect to see in most large GAA club grounds on a Saturday morning. Organised mayhem. A few different fields were set out side by side with small goals and about 20 kids chasing the same ball in the same direction on each. Headless chickens that couldn't have been happier with themselves. It was heart-warming, hilarious, and I imagined incredibly frustrating for any aspiring coach. Baby steps, though.

On the side field, Paraic was winding up the football and the kids were eyeing up the hurleys that had been lined up along the sidelines. There was saliva dripping down the sides of their mouths, and their coach realised their minds were now completely incapable of thinking about anything else. A few of the kids had been nagging him to take sticks home with them from previous drill session, but he had held tough in the hope of securing the few camáns he had. This would be the first time he would be introducing the ash to the youngsters on a large scale: the first underage hurling training session in Singapore.

I positioned myself behind the main goals, as I watched the 20 or so players puc the ball to one another across the field. Some were only finding their feet with basics such as the grip, but some of them had taken to the game like ducks to water. One pair in particular grabbed my attention. A 12-year-old English kid in a Rangers jersey was striking left and right out of his hands and off the ground across the field to another pre-teen in a Celtic jersey. My, how far we've come.

Just as I was getting lost in my own little transfixed world, watching two joy-filled kids knocking a ball around, happy as can be, an errant sliotar came flying in my direction. I caught its flight at the last second from the corner of my eye and just managed to duck out of its way. I should have stayed where I was and taken one for the team. There were five of us looking for that ball in a bush for the next half-hour. Sadly, we never found it. But what would a Sunday morning hurling training session be without a couple of aul fellas in wellies scouring the bushes for an errant brand-new ball? Ah, felt just like home.

After a good hour and a half, we climbed back into Paraic's car and headed for his house, where we were to meet Peter Ryan. Originally from the Synge Street area of Dublin, Ryan was the secretary of the Asian Board, but he was also heavily involved in the Gaelic Lions GAA club. He and Paraic became good friends after they had met in Japan some years before and had founded the Japan GAA club in Tokyo before moving on to Singapore with work. The two lads were keeping tabs on the kids as we settled down for breakfast. The smell of sizzling Galtee rashers would lift you. The kids, meanwhile, bundles of energy, seemed keen to take a dip in the backyard swimming pool. It was a warm and balmy day, and it certainly seemed like a good idea to me. Given half a chance. 'Tis far from post-training-session Sunday morning dips in the outdoor pool most young hurlers are reared. Many would be lucky if the hose in the field had strength to splash the muck off.

Peter and Paraic eventually caved and the kids headed off to don their swimming gear as the adults started to chat about my adventures. By now, there was a plateful of Galtee sausages and rashers in the middle of the table and I was struggling to finish sentences. There'd be no more talking for at least ten minutes. I hadn't seen a proper sausage in nearly two months.

After a sinful amount of pork, we sat back with a pot of Barry's and I began to query the lads about their background. Paraic was originally from Mayo, but he lived in Dublin for a number of years while he trained to become a teacher. Peter, on the other hand, had been born and raised in the capital. They had known each other now for several years, since that first chance meeting in Tokyo. Sensing a shared Dublin experience, and a subject in common to all participants, I began to tell the lads about my own club, Lucan Sarsfields, and about our failure to win a senior championship of any description since our formation in 1886. Paraic consoles me with his own tale of woe. Apparently, he had lost a Dublin under-21 football championship final in 1989 when he was playing with Erin's Hope (the club team from the primary school teacher-training college St Patrick's in Drumcondra). They had beaten St Vincent's and UCD along the way but had fallen short. Even all these years later the wounds were still fresh. Peter's ears pricked up at the story. With a look of astonishment, he jumped in to say that he had actually played in a Dublin under-21 football championship semi-final in 1989 with Templeogue Synge Street. Against Erin's Hope. Half a decade of friendship, with daily talk of GAA, and this subject had only just come up for the first time. I sat back amazed at what was transpiring in front of me. One full-back, one full-forward. Turned out the two boys had marked each other that day all those years ago. Small, small, small aul world.

After breakfast Paraic dropped me back into the city with some details on the Asian Games festival the club had hosted a few months previously at the Polo Grounds. It had been one of the biggest and best-run events in Asian GAA history and, according to some senior GAA figures, had rivalled many other events in North America and Britain. The people of the Gaelic Lions were understandably proud of how well everything had gone. They had secured promotional airtime on the local television station before the event and had even made the nightly news during the event itself. Singapore had already hosted two previous All Stars tours, but this had been by far their biggest undertaking.

The Asian Games were in their 12th year and had attracted to Singapore almost 500 players in forty-eight teams from ten countries. Sides from Shanghai, Beijing, Shenzhen, Dalian, Taiwan, Hong Kong, Dubai, Japan, Korea and Singapore had been joined by new teams from Malaysia, Thailand and Vietnam for the football and hurling competitions. It had been a massive success and had, rather encouragingly, continued its growth from the previous year's tournament in Shanghai. Most years Micháel Ó Muircheartaigh came out to do the commentary for the Games, but he had been unavailable the previous June and so the honours had fallen to his son, Cormac, who worked as a doctor in Singapore and who was also a long-time member of the Gaelic Lions. According to all available reports, he certainly hadn't disgraced the family name on the microphone.

For now, the Gaelic Lions were just concentrating on the basics. Bringing the underage kids through was a big priority, and Croke Park had been good in helping out, especially through programmes such as the Go-Games (an innovative new underage format designed to hone the football and hurling skills of kids ten years old and younger), which have proven such a huge success back home.

After a quick change and a shower, I was off to watch the club's senior footballers being put through their paces. It was a dirty, mucky Sunday afternoon at the SMU Training Pitch, where the Lions do their adult training sessions. Both the men's and women's football teams had been strong for several years, but it was still early in the season and the numbers were low. About 30 players showed up to tread water in the slop, as the women and men were mixed together for a quick game. I took my seat safely in the dry and comfortable surrounds of a small grandstand that sat alongside the pitch. In almost every way, it reminded me of a junior C football training session on a dark and wet January night with the season still months away. The only difference being that this actually looked like fun.

After an hour or so of watching the lads splash away and struggle to even bounce the ball, it was time for me to take my leave. I said my goodbyes and headed to the top of the road to flag down a taxi. I was hungry, cold, wet and tired but invigorated by what I'd seen, not just in Singapore but all over the continent of Asia. I'd miss it, but I really hoped that I'd be back someday soon.

The Asian Games are renowned as being home to the single best weekend of craic anywhere on the planet each and every year. Hopefully, I'd get to experience that for myself one day in the future. For now, though, I was getting my passport together for phase two of my little adventure. G'day, Australia.

AUSTRALASIA

9

THE SATURDAY CLUB

MONDAY, 12 NOVEMBER 2007 – SYDNEY

'To leave home is to die a little, partings can be sad, with fear always in the old people's mind: "Will we ever see him again?" Often, they never do.'

– Kerry Murphy's Memoirs:
The Diaries of an Irish Immigrant

After almost two months of trekking through Asia – and changing currencies, languages and customs on an almost weekly basis – it was a relief to be back in what felt like the normal world again. They say familiarity breeds contempt, but Australia, and particularly Sydney, is a very warm and welcoming place. Especially for a weary traveller. The funds were low and the tank was running close to empty, but the plan had been to recharge in Sydney for a few months before heading off on the final leg of the trip through New Zealand and America. My three friends were still trekking through the jungles of Laos as I landed in the New South Wales capital, but the idea was to get a place of our own when they arrived. For the time being, though, I was staying with a few friends in Bondi Junction. Hedonism central.

It's very easy to get settled in Sydney. The tricky part, I had been told before I'd left Ireland, was leaving the place. How true that would turn out to be. But for the moment I was still in holiday mode and keen to get my bearings.

Bondi Junction is the famous eastern Sydney suburb where the backpacker hordes gather en masse. Especially the Irish ones. It's about two miles from Bondi Beach and it also houses the biggest shopping centre in the Eastern Suburbs, the Westfield, as well as two of the biggest Irish pubs in the city. It's not long before the Tea Gardens and the Cock 'n Bull become a home away from home.

Unfortunately, my timing was slightly off, as per usual, and I'd missed two of the biggest events of the 2007 calendar. The Melbourne Cup had been run nine days before I landed and I'd also missed the Australasian State GAA Games, which had been held in Sydney in October. Teams from Queensland, Victoria, Western Australia, South Australia, Tasmania and Wellington and Auckland in New Zealand had travelled for the event, and I was sick to have missed out. Can't be everywhere, I suppose.

It doesn't take long to acclimatise to life in Sydney, but the beer can claim you early on if you're not careful. Many inter-county hurlers and footballers have passed through the city over the years and not managed to make it out of the pub long enough to grace the playing fields. Many would have come intending to travel all over the continent in their year out but wouldn't even leave New South Wales. Sydney can be seriously addictive. I was determined not to let that happen to us, though. Whatever happened, I'd hurl.

By the end of the week, Ger, Mark and Joey had landed with two of our other friends from home, Joey Byrne and Tommy Somers. We grabbed a hostel for a few weeks in the Surry Hills area of the Eastern Suburbs in the upstairs of a pub called the Bat & Ball. The hostel sits on a busy crossroads in a place called Moore Park, just across from the Sydney Cricket Ground (home of the Sydney Swans) and the Sydney Football Stadium, where the NSW Waratahs rugby union team, the Sydney Roosters rugby league team and Sydney FC play their home games. However, I also learned that the area had been the original home of the GAA in Sydney.

* * *

In 1951, the first modern Gaelic Games came to Moore Park. The first-ever inter-state games were held there when a team from Melbourne came up to visit and take on the first-ever New South Wales team in the September of that year. A tradition began and, from there, has never died.

Evidence of Gaelic Games on Australian soil can actually be traced back much further. Australasian County Board secretary Gerard Roe, a full-time employee of the GAA, who now calls Alice Springs home, has found reports of exhibition games during St Patrick's Day celebrations dating back to before the turn of the century; in fact, even as far back as the 1840s and '50s down in Victoria. Clubs with names such as Michael Davitt's, Tempe, Surry Hills, Redfern and Paddington lined out to hurl in Moore Park on a regular basis. From that point, there was a lull and only the odd sighting of regular games could be traced – broken up by the two world wars, for the most part. But from the post-Second World War era onwards, the GAA began to take root in New South Wales, and also in Victoria in particular. The age of the GAA in Australia had begun in earnest.

The resurgence didn't happen on its own, of course. As is always the case, such things take dedicated people willing to go the extra mile. In the case of the New South Wales GAA, one of those shining lights was a man by the name of Kerry Murphy. A son of Knocknagoshel, near Castleisland in Co. Kerry, Murphy came to Australia in 1950 and immediately got involved with the local GAA. His love affair began in a guesthouse in Enmore, just up the road from where we were staying, where a gang of other Irish lads were staying with a woman known only as Mrs O'Flaherty. Murphy quickly heard of a game taking place in Moore Park one Sunday morning. From there, he was hooked. That's not to say Murphy was the single driving force behind the success story that became the GAA in New South Wales. Far from it. What he is, though, is a fine example of a man willing to put in the hard, thankless hours behind the scenes. His book, *Kerry Murphy's Memoirs: Diary of an Irish Immigrant*, offered me an invaluable insight into the life of an

Irishman abroad in the '50s, '60s and '70s – and in particular of an Irishman in Sydney. It certainly proved a decent starting point.

After his first experience at Moore Park, the hunger continued to rise within Murphy. He quickly set about forming a team of his own and began by holding a meeting between all the residents of Mrs O'Flaherty's guesthouse. From there, the Newtown Shamrocks were founded. It was just the beginning of a long life of dedication from the Kerryman (he was of good pedigree, having played in an All-Ireland junior football championship semi-final for Kerry against Leitrim in the mid-'40s). His efforts were duly noted and he was rewarded, being asked to manage the touring All-Australian team that hit the shores of Ireland in 1978. (He also colourfully recalls being approached by an Aussie Rules scout after one particular game at the All-Australian Games in Melbourne in 1952.) The highest honour and recognition available within the GAA in NSW – life membership – was also bestowed upon him in 1977. It was a golden age for the GAA in New South Wales back then and Murphy was at the heart of it.

For me and the lads, though, we already had in mind a club to join. A friend of ours, Aidan Glover, had lived in Sydney a few years earlier and had hurled with the Craobh Pádraig club. He had given us a number for the club's main man, a Wexford native by the name of Shane O'Brien, and we were just about to give him a call in late November when Joey got a text through on his Irish phone. A former underage Dublin hurling colleague of his, Mick Fogarty from the Finagallians club, had heard about our arrival and had been quickly dispatched on recruiting duty. He'd been here for the past two years and had hurled for the Sydney Shamrocks since his arrival. He told us that the club were due to hold a 'booze cruise' in a few weeks' time and that we should come along and meet the lads. We didn't need to be asked twice. It was only December and the season wouldn't start until March, so we bought our tickets from Mick and a few weeks later headed for Rose Bay wharf to board the boat.

* * *

One o'clock on a Sunday afternoon in January and there were some seriously sore-looking heads knocking around the place. With the boat loaded up with a wall of beer and cider, we pulled away and the DJ on board kicked into full flow. The boat was packed with potential hurlers, current hurlers, non-hurlers and those just along for the ride. The craic was unbelievable and after four hours floating around Sydney harbour the Shamrocks had our vote. This was our kind of club. And for the next few months at least, it *would* be our club.

SUNDAY, 27 JANUARY 2008

By late January, the GAA season was once again sneaking up on the Gaels of New South Wales. It was midsummer and the heat was almost smothering at times, but the clubs were back in training. Some elder statesmen were well acclimatised to the heat; others would never quite get used to it. Nonetheless, most of the clubs had been back on the fields of Centennial Park since the first few weeks of the new year. The large throngs of holidaying backpackers that littered the city for Christmas, St Stephen's Day and New Year's Eve had, for the most part, moved on to climates new. Many others had said their farewells to Australia altogether and headed back to Ireland, but a core of Irishmen and women remains as the seasons come and go. Some will never leave.

Australia Day weekend was now upon us. It had been nearly a month since the hedonistic 'orphan' holidays of the Christmas season, as they're known locally. It had been a busy month. Bondi Beach was packed to the rafters with the usual sight of Paddies in Santa hats on Christmas Day, despite the unseasonal cold. St Stephen's Day had seen thousands of Irish visitors pack the stands at Randwick Racecourse for international passport day – when, if you show your international passport on the day, you get complimentary entry. And the last of the fireworks left over from New Year's Eve had blazed their way into the night sky in celebration of Australia's national day. It had been a heavy few weeks and we were keen to get back to some training. If nothing else, just to run the beer out of ourselves.

The Shamrocks had been easing back into training with a session per week on a Saturday afternoon in Centennial Park. The heat was unmerciful, though. It wasn't like the Phoenix Park, or somewhere at home where there are goalposts as far as the eye can see. It was laps (two for warm-up), a few drills and straight into a match with jumpers for goalposts. Simple as, no messing. And literally jumpers.

We were enjoying getting ourselves back into the swing of things, though, and getting to know a few of the lads on the team a little better. The boys roaring out the orders were getting to know us, too.

Mark Tobin from Mungret in Limerick and Declan Maher from Shinrone in Offaly had been running the club for the past few years since Nicky Murphy, from Carrickshock in Kilkenny, packed up shop and headed for home. Murphy had founded the club back in 1997 with Larry Delahunty and Harry Dermody on board, as well as former National Hurling League-winning Kilkenny captain Bill Hennessy. Both Tobin and Maher had played representative hurling for NSW for years in the State Games. Tobin was the onfield general, while Maher was the brains behind the operation on the sidelines (although he still played a little when he was needed). Indeed, the two lads had been at home in Kilkenny a few weeks before for the tenth anniversary of the club. Tobin had been named as the only player still hurling for the club to make the team of the decade – a serious achievement considering what had been through there. A special booklet had been produced for the anniversary event and Maher had secured a copy of it for me.

The founding fathers of the club, and in particular Hennessy, had hurled with the storied club of Central Coast before jumping ship to the Shamrocks, according to the introduction. Since then more than 30 titles had been won. The name of Kieren Murphy, from St Finnbarr's in Cork, of the 1998 team, jumped off the pages at me straight away. From the 2001 team list, I spotted a man from my own club in Martin O'Halloran, while the goalkeeper on that same team was a Wexford man named Anthony Rochford, whom I would hurl junior alongside with Lucan a few years later after he'd returned home from Oz. I've said it before, I'll say it again. Small, small world.

We were cooling down after a tougher than usual evening session as Maher pulled a large cooler out from the back of his van alongside the pitch. We'd long since run out of water, but needless to say the cooler wasn't for the H_2O. It was full of beer and cider, some of the leftovers from the booze cruise. We dug in, delighted with ourselves. It might have only been January, and for the moment the pressure was off, but the serious business was just around the corner. There wouldn't be beers after training all season long. Not for most of the panel, anyway.

SUNDAY, 23 MARCH 2008 – GOSFORD, NSW

After a few months of hard yakka on the fields of Centennial Park, the first real event of the season had finally arrived. The annual Central Coast tournament in Gosford is regarded as second only to the championship in the prestige stakes in the NSW neck of the woods. The Shamrocks had won it for the past number of years and the boys were keen to keep that recent domination going. It was mainly because of the quality of player that it seemed to attract that Gosford was so highly regarded. In a city like Sydney, where so many backpackers are only just passing through, it's hard to keep the steady nucleus of a squad together. Most backpackers tend to call Sydney home from November through to the start of April or so before moving on, and so the backbones of the clubs are the permanent residents and the people who have landed four-year visa sponsorships from local companies. The odd backpacker will sometimes hang around for a full year, but on the whole they come and go and scatter themselves across the continent. For Gosford, however, it was all hands on deck from far and wide.

We'd had a steady number of over-25 players at our sessions for the previous few weeks in the lead-up to Gosford, so as we pulled up to the meeting point at the Cock 'n Bull in Bondi Junction at 7 a.m. we were surprised to see a bus that could hold about 50 people sitting waiting for us. Turns out, we'd need it.

By this stage in our travels, we'd been joined by another Lucan colleague of ours, Kevin Roche, but he wasn't the only new face we could see as we looked around. Former players whom we hadn't yet met had flown in from Perth, Melbourne and elsewhere to play for the team in the annual tournament. This was serious business. It was a 15-a-side blitz tournament, but we would have as many lads on the sideline as on the field all day long.

We didn't have much time to look around and smell the roses, though. Our first game was against the club's most heated rivals: a 9 a.m. throw-in against Shane O'Brien's Craobh Pádraig. The morning dew was finally shaken from its slumber as the ball was thrown in at around 9.15 a.m. Those of us new to the rivalries of NSW hurling were told this might not be a pretty sight. Understatement of the year. We'd duly get hammered off the park by a Pat's team who had been 15 minutes late in showing up. Walking off the field at 10 a.m. with our tails firmly between our legs, we found ourselves wishing they hadn't bothered showing up at all.

The football tournament was in full swing on the other field as we grabbed some food along the sidelines and awaited our second and final group game against Sydney's biggest club, Michael Cusack's. We had a long break between our first and second games and so decided to take in some of the big ball as we mulled over just what had gone wrong against the Pat's. Six teams were taking part in the football, with Cormac McAnallen's, Young Irelands, Clan na Gael, Michael Cusack's and Penrith Gaels from Sydney being joined for the weekend by the Wolfe Tones club from Melbourne. In the women's football competition, Clan na Gael went on to beat McAnallen's, while hosts Central Coast beat Pat's in the camogie decider.

The Shamrocks were still alive in the hurling. Just about. Raginghot favourites Central Coast had beaten Cusack's and St Pat's, and in a quirky twist of fate it was possible we would still reach the final against the hosts if we could beat Cusack's by 13 points or more. Like men possessed, the three-in-a-row Gosford bid somehow found life. We won by 15 and set up a decider against the Coast.

The Craobh Pádraig players, mentors and supporters who had lined the field to watch the game were less than amused by what had transpired. Little we could do about it, though. You can only beat what's put in front of you.

Confidence soaring, and the sun at its highest point in the sky, the words were heated from Tobin in the pre-match warm-up behind the goals. We were foaming at the mouth. Our captain for the day, Davy Carter from the Young Ireland's club in Kilkenny, was due to head home to Ireland for good the following week. Do it for Davy, boys, was the message. Do it for Davy. Unfortunately for our bubbling adrenaline, the start of the final was delayed at the last minute. A pair of overly eager footballers had been kicking around in the goalmouth and taking shots at one another when one of them felt it might be a good idea to jump up and hang off the crossbar. Of course, crossbars aren't built for such acts of buffoonery. The timber had duly snapped right in the middle and that tribal fervour we'd built in the warm-up began to fade as we waited for the quick-fix job on the goalposts. A broken hurley stick was affixed to join the broken pieces together and we were soon ready to get it going. Ingenious stuff altogether.

The Coast ran out to an early lead, as we struggled to regain our concentration. Their corner-forward had been terrorising teams all day long, but after a shaky start we managed to keep him under wraps and pull away into a solid lead. With two minutes left, we were up by five points. It was ours to lose. Then Coast struck for a controversial goal. There was a huge crowd gathered on the sideline and the grandstand finish was set up. Coast came with one last surge, an all-out assault on our besieged defence, which by now had 14 men inside the 21. But it was too late for Coast. It was all over. The Shamrocks had won their third Gosford title in a row and, somehow, I'd managed to win a medal on a third continent. Result.

After the ceremonies and a rousing speech from our departing captain, we hit the showers before heading across to catch the end of the men's football final. Wolfe Tones proved too strong for a McAnallen's team that included an All-Ireland medal winners amongst its ranks – Tyrone's Owen Bradley. Tones were the first team from Melbourne to visit, and so to find themselves with winners' medals in their pockets was a massive bonus. They were understandably in the mood for celebrating. Obviously, so were we.

The two-hour journey back to the Cock 'n Bull felt somewhat shorter, especially considering we now had medals and a trophy weighing us down. Maher – or 'Fleece', as he was known to everyone – had stocked the bus with about five crates of beer and six boxes of Magners cider. Spirits were high and it wasn't long before the microphone was being passed from hand to hand. The bus was rocking to the sound of Irish ballads and one particularly brilliant improvised Sydney Shamrocks cover of a Christy Moore classic, 'Shamrocks Go To Gosford'. Boy, did we ever. There was even a mobile call to Ireland fed into the speaker system, as Nicky Murphy passed his congratulations from home in Kilkenny. This is what it was all about.

Back at the Cock 'n Bull, it wasn't long before things started getting a little wild. The Bondi pub sponsor the Shamrocks, and they supply the fingerfood as we supply the atmosphere. It was a long night for everyone, and in most parts a little hazy. Somewhere along the line the trophy went missing, too. We were sure it would turn up. Could have been worse, could have had to get up for work in the morning.

MONDAY, 24 MARCH 2008

One of the better singers on the bus had been Johnny Brennan from Balbriggan. He'd left us early into the Sunday night session to make sure he got up the following morning for his new job.

The rest of us had powered through to the neighbouring bar, the Tea Gardens, the following day, and there were about 30 of us in the corner as Johnny rocked in around noon. He'd shown up for work that morning, fresh and on time, but had been told his services would no longer be required. He'd missed the session of the year for a job that hadn't even existed. A stinger of seriously epic proportions.

About an hour later we noticed the Wolfe Tones boys from Victoria on the other side of the bar in full flow. In fairness, most of us would make it up for work the following morning, but I'd later hear that half the Tones lads would go on to miss their flight to Melbourne. Some of them wouldn't get even home until the following weekend. That's what Sydney can do to you sometimes. As I keep saying, some people never leave the place. All the same, you wouldn't change it for the world.

TUESDAY, 25 MARCH 2008

Tuesday morning was a delicate operation for most of us. I'd taken the Monday off work and was glad of it, but I was even more glad of the job I'd secured for myself. The *Irish Echo* in Sydney is the only Irish newspaper in Australia and the editor, owner and founder of the operation is a Meath man by the name of Billy Cantwell. Part of my work with the paper was to look after the sports section and it was a thrill to have the opportunity to get to know the GAA heads over the course of the upcoming season through my work there. One of the first acts on the Tuesday, of course, was making sure that someone sent me in a picture of the victorious Shamrocks from Gosford the Sunday before.

There was a lot to learn. The GAA in Australia is an altogether different animal to that in Asia and the Gulf – there's no shortage of expats knocking around the place and the history is rich and old.

I wasn't quite sure what I expected to find on my first day out at the GAA grounds in Auburn, but I did know that Sydney is the biggest population centre in the country and also the biggest

GAA area, so I suspected there would be a fairly sizable crowd and top-notch facilities to boot. Sadly, I discovered that the New South Wales GAA is not quite as well equipped as I'd imagined.

The committee had just elected a new chairman in the form of Corkman Brian Deane and one of my early tasks was to interview him about his plans for the year ahead. It would turn out to be a bumper year for the GAA in Sydney, with a touring Irish International Rules team coming to visit in November. It should have been a field day.

The fundamental issue in Sydney is the playing field. The NSW GAA rent a field from Auburn Council around half an hour west of the city. Princes Park is not owned by the GAA but merely leased, and it's shared with a local cricket club. It has a canteen, dressing-room facilities and all that jazz, but the field is awkward to get to and in the middle of the field there's a rock hard (except when wet, when it turns into quicksand) cricket pitch. Makes for some shocking hops.

I was confused as to how the GAA had ended up out there, but apparently a large number of Irish people lived out that way in years gone by, though this is no longer the case. The numbers playing GAA in Sydney should have been far stronger than they were, especially considering the number of young people who called the city home for six months or so. So many backpackers – many of them talented GAA people at home in Ireland – would pass through the city each year without ever having lifted a hurl or kicked a ball. A lot of that was down to being in 'holiday mode', of course, but the sheer logistics of just getting out to the field each Sunday was also a major factor.

The backpackers – and therefore most of the twenty-something footballers and hurlers – live in the Eastern Suburbs of the city. Most of them don't have cars. To get from Bondi Junction to Princes Park on a Sunday morning requires a twenty-minute train ride to Central Station in the city, a forty-minute or so train to Auburn and then a ten-minute taxi ride to the pitch. For a 10 a.m. throw-in, you'd need to be up near 7 a.m. And you'd be $20 lighter as a result of it. Not much to many people, but to a generation of flat-broke Irishmen and women in their 20s, surviving on noodles and boxed wine, it was somewhat of a hindrance. Most backpackers on a year out tended not to find the prospect of Sunday morning GAA all that appealing as a result, and so the numbers had been dwindling.

That year alone the association had lost an entire club in the form of the Irish Rovers. Only eight clubs remained in NSW – Michael Cusack's, Clan na Gael, Cormac McAnallen's, Craobh Pádraig, Penrith Gaels, Central Coast, Deane's club Young Ireland's and, of course, the Sydney Shamrocks. The future of the association really hung in the balance, if you looked at it in the cold light of day.

There have been record numbers of young Irish people moving to Sydney in recent years as the Irish economy continues to weaken. Australia offers an increasingly appealing alternative to the persistent uncertainty of the Irish job market – especially as it continues to be gripped by an ever-increasing skills shortage. Ireland has the skills, Australia has the jobs. And the weather. A growing Irish population can only be good for the association there. The key, however, is making sure they join the GAA.

Outside of its current problems, which I'm sure the NSW GAA shares with many others, I was intrigued by the history of Gaelic games there and soon set about learning what I could about how it all began. Some things come as very little surprise to me – the fundamentals of the GAA are basically the same everywhere you go. It's an amateur organisation that relies on the goodwill and volunteer efforts of many to keep it alive. In that regard, the GAA abroad is similar in many ways to the association at home at grassroots level. Money doesn't grow on trees and that's why sponsorship events, and particularly patrons, are so vital to everything that happens in the GAA world outside Europe. Croke Park provide practically nothing to these clubs, yet they survive. Nothing has changed on that front since 1950. Not since then has a year gone by Down Under where an All-Australasian Games festival has not been held – and there's only been one in which Victoria was not involved.

New South Wales's greatest rivals have always fought them toe-to-toe and a great rivalry has grown between the two biggest states over the past sixty or so years. The first All-Australian Games were held in NSW in 1951 and the following year a team from Sydney travelled to St Kilda in Melbourne for the renewal. There was a great hunger back then for such a unifying Irish festival event and those games in St Kilda were thronged with people who came from far and wide to enjoy the Irish dancing and music, as well as the football and hurling. Amazingly, over 15,000 reportedly attended the football final that year. You'd do well to see that in Croker on St Patrick's Day some years. Every second year the games swapped between Melbourne and Sydney until 1964, when the scope of the GAA internationally was changed for ever.

On 8 September, the first-ever overseas visitors came to Australia, as NSW welcomed the New York GAA to the Erskineville Oval just outside Sydney. The improved technology in transportation had made international travel, even to places as isolated as Australia, much, much easier. Even within the country planes changed everything. It's sometimes hard to fathom, but Australia is quite simply massive. Perth is actually further away from Sydney than Dublin is from Moscow. Long drive, that. And so the increasing availability of air travel was the key to growing the GAA countrywide, and particularly the level of competition that existed inter-state.

In 1965, the All-Australian Games grew beyond the heated rivalry of Victoria and New South Wales. For the first time, there was a new kid in town, as the newly formed GAA of South Australia were primed to land in Sydney. The games continued to grow from there, and in 1967 another huge step was taken, as South Australia held their first-ever All-Australian Games in Adelaide.

Many things were beginning to change. The GAA was fast becoming a force to be reckoned with on a national level, and the Aussies were beginning to take notice. In their minds, this Gaelic football business looked a bit like Aussie Rules. Questions inevitably arise about the origins of Australian Rules football when talking about the GAA in an Australian context. It's an issue of some debate

Down Under, but the general consensus is that Aussie Rules is quite simply a bastardised version of Gaelic football played with a rugby ball on a cricket pitch. It's the most compelling argument as far as theories of origin go (although in one particularly eye-opening pub conversation in Melbourne, a high-ranking GAA official did theorise aloud that Gaelic football had, in fact, learned more from Aussie Rules than the other way around).

In a more modern context, however, the criss-cross between Gaelic football players and Aussie Rules footballers can be traced back to 1968, when Meath's All-Ireland-winning team embarked on a tour of Australia. Kerry Murphy managed the NSW team that took on the champions under floodlights at the Redfern Oval that year, but his highlight, and that of many others, would have come in 1970, when all-conquering All-Ireland champions Kerry followed Meath's lead and took flight on a tour to Australia. The seeds had been sown with these two tours, with Aussie Rules scouts in attendance at games on both tours, even way back then. The spark had lit the flames of friendship, however uneasy at times, between the AFL and the GAA.

The year 1973 was huge for the association, with Queensland, Western Australia and Auckland all coming on board, but the international dimension was also really beginning to take hold. The big names continued to arrive in their droves to the shores of Botany Bay (the site of Sydney's international airport). Later that same eventful year, New York rolled into town with one of the most star-studded line-ups – in both codes – ever to grace a field outside of an All Stars game. John 'Kerry' O'Donnell, the driving force behind the GAA in the Big Apple, had brought with him Christy Ring and Ollie Walsh in the hurling, and Mick O'Connell and Niall Sheehy in the football. The New Yorkers travelled all over the continent, even making time to visit the lads of the New Zealand GAA along the way. For many people who had moved to Australia so many years before, this was a special occasion. Many thought they'd never again set eyes on the likes of Ring or O'Connell in the flesh. One can only imagine what something like that would have meant to them. And to the GAA in Australia as a whole.

From that point, it was milestone after milestone. In 1975, Western Australia held their first Games in Perth; in 1976, the first game of ladies' football was played at a picnic event; the following year, Brisbane held the National Games for the first time. The first-ever underage games were also played at the event that year, with many of the three teams made up largely of locally born boys and girls. In 1978, the first-ever All-Australian team left for their tour of the world (going through New York, London, Cork, Clare, Belfast, Meath and then on to the hallowed soil of Croke Park to take on an Aer Lingus selection) with Murphy at the helm – a long way from his first sojourns onto the fields of Moore Park in 1950. This was progress on an unprecedented level.

The 1980 State Games in Sydney were notable for not only the debut appearance of New Zealand but also the fact that the finals were shown on Australian television for the first time. RTÉ commentator Michael O'Hehir even made an appearance. All the while, though, the Aussies were watching.

It was in 1980 that the crossover between the AFL and GAA really began. The three-in-a-row All-Ireland-winning Kerry team (soon to be four in a row) had come to Australia, touring Melbourne, Sydney, Adelaide and Perth, and the AFL clubs had come knocking. The Aussie Rules scouts were seeing at first hand what was arguably the best Gaelic football team ever assembled and they couldn't help but be excited by what they saw. The potential for Irish players to succeed in the AFL was plain for all to see – and not just the potential of what they could see in front of them, but the potential of generations of Gaelic footballers to come.

Aussie Rules scouts and Gaelic football talent go way further back than the current crop that have enraged GAA communities across the land in Ireland in recent years. The 'Irish experiment', as it's known in AFL circles Down Under, had been born with these touring county sides, but it wouldn't begin to flow in earnest until the turn of the century.

China Champions: The Shenzhen Celts (me: back row, right) celebrate with the All-China Games men's football Bowl trophy after beating Beijing in Dalian, north-east China, September 2007.

China Syndrome: The Shenzhen Celts football team – (second left) Alan Cuddihy, Sean Chang, Joe Perrott, me, Mikey Barry and Josh Bizmanovsky (front) – celebrate after our All-China Games victory in Dalian. This photo was taken in Genghis Khan's Mongolian Barbecue, a giant revolving restaurant in the middle of the city built in the shape of a giant football.

Singapore Training: The youngsters of the Gaelic Lions at the first-ever underage hurling training to be held in Singapore. The session took place at the out-of-use Turf City horse-racing track. I had a front-row seat on this historic day for the Lion Cubs in November 2007.

Mac Attack: Former Derry star Joe Brolly and former Tyrone defender Chris Lawn get ready for action in the colours of the Cormac McAnallen's GAA club from Sydney, who took on the Aidan McAnespie's club from Boston in Aghaloo in Co. Tyrone in February 2008. The game was organised to mark the 20th anniversary of the death of 24-year-old Aidan McAnespie, who was shot dead on his way to a GAA game in 1988. (Picture courtesy of Cormac McAnallen's GAC)

Gosford Goalposts: The makeshift fix job on the goalposts at the Central Coast tournament in March 2008. An overly eager football player had snapped the crossbar in two shortly before the hurling final, but the two shattered halves were ingeniously put back together using a piece of broken hurley stick.

Gosford Champions: Joey Byrne, Kevin Roche, Declan Maher, Mick Fogarty, me and Róisín Hayden from the Sydney Shamrocks celebrate with the 2008 Central Coast hurling tournament trophy at the Cock 'n Bull in Sydney's Bondi Junction after winning the event in Gosford, March 2008.

Victorious Victorians: Ultan Browne and Mick Finn of the Sinn Féin GAA club in Melbourne hold aloft the men's senior football league trophy in August 2008 at Gaelic Park in Keysborough. (Picture courtesy of Darryl Kennedy)

Peter the Great: Tyrone legend Peter Canavan, who was visiting Sydney for a charity event being run by Cormac McAnallen's GAA club, presents Clan na Gael captain Norma Kelly with the ladies' senior football championship trophy at Auburn, August 2008. (Picture courtesy of Pearl Phelan)

Cusack's Joy: NSW GAA chairman Brian Deane looks on as victorious Michael Cusack's captain Donal O'Leary lifts the NSW senior hurling championship trophy, August 2008. (Picture courtesy of Pearl Phelan)

Under Construction: How Treasure Island, home of the San Francisco GAA, looked from the air, September 2008. The new grounds were ready in time to host the GAA All Stars football game just three months later.

Treasure Island: The GAA grounds, with the Bay Bridge in the background, September 2008.

Treasure Island: GAA President Nickey Brennan officially opens Páirc na nGael, the new home of the GAA on the west coast of America, December 2008. Brennan was in attendance as part of the All Stars tour to the Bay Area of California.

Tribal Quest: Galway and Ireland star Michael Meehan – who took over the goalkeeping duties for Meath's David Gallagher during Ireland's friendly game against a NSW selection in Sydney in November 2008 – poses for a picture with young fans and NSW player Richard Moylette. (Picture courtesy of Martin Brady)

Garden Party: NSW and Cormac McAnallen's player John Brophy with young Wicklow fan Paudie Ó Dálaigh meet Wicklow and Ireland star Leighton Glynn at the challenge game between a NSW selection and Ireland in Sydney on 2 November 2008. Glynn would fly home the following day to hurl for his club, Glenealy, in the Wicklow county final replay. (Picture courtesy of Martin Brady)

Cal Bears: San Francisco GAA PRO Liam Reidy with his son, Shane, at the first-ever colleges hurling game between the University of California, Berkeley, and Stanford in San Francisco, January 2009.

Stanford Hurlers: The Stanford University hurling team that took part in that first-ever colleges hurling match in San Francisco, January 2009.

For all those still bemoaning the loss of talented youth to the AFL, just remember that it could have been an awful lot worse had it started years earlier. Tadhg Kennelly was really the first of that new generation of Gaelic footballers to be lured from under the nose of the GAA. (In a contemporary context, at least. Dubliner Jim Stynes had paved the way for Tadhg and others like him when he left for Melbourne in the 1980s, as part of the Irish experiment.) An emerging star on the Kerry minor football team and son of Kingdom legend Tim Kennelly, Tadhg had called Sydney home since he was a teenager, winning an AFL Premiership (the only Irishman ever to have done so) and numerous other accolades along the way. Stynes had become the most-successful-ever Gaelic football convert by winning the Brownlow Medal (Aussie Rules' highest individual playing honour) back in 1991 with the Melbourne Demons. After Stynes, there had been a lull, but Kennelly's success at the Sydney Swans had opened the floodgates once more. At one point in late 2008, there would be an astonishing eleven Irish players on the books of AFL clubs. Who knew where it might end.

SUNDAY, 6 APRIL 2008

It had been two weeks since our triumph in Gosford and we hadn't quite managed to run all the beer out of our systems. I was due to make my first visit to Auburn as a player, but the Shamrocks were not really relishing the task of taking on a wounded Central Coast team in our first league game. Training hadn't been quite as hardcore in the previous few weeks as it had been in the lead-up to Gosford. You got the impression the Coast had been working hard, though.

Our squad had settled down since a few of the Gosford number had returned to the warmer climes of Perth and Brisbane, but the core of the squad was still strong. There were a few of us who knew we were unlikely to figure in the starting XV with any sort of regularity – there's All-Ireland club medals on the panel, for crying out loud. We were still determined to train hard, though. There's nothing better than a puc about in the sunshine on a Saturday afternoon to keep the liver fresh and to sweat out the evils of the night before.

Coast would duly hammer the living daylights out of us in that opening league game, but it mattered little in the grand scheme of things. The league was just the league – at that stage of the year, anyway. Tobin consoled us in the dressing-room that there was a long year ahead. Indeed, we'd have to play the Coast again – as well as Cusack's and Craobh Pádraig twice each in the group stages – before any sort of quarter-final or semi-final draw was contemplated. There are only four hurling clubs in Sydney, so you get to know one another quite well over the course of the year. Adds to the niggle.

Like any good fringe players, those of us on the outs of the starting team talk a mighty game – so much so that we would eventually decide to make a game of it. A group of us had taken Mark's words to heart and decided not to take the league too seriously. We resolved instead to ease ourselves into the long season ahead with regular post-training pints on a Saturday afternoon. Kevin Roche, J.J. Haren and Brian O'Keeffe from Ballygunner in Waterford, our new friend Mick Fogarty from Fingallians and the team's number-one sideline man, Eddie Butler from Piltown, would stroll our way down Oxford Street from Centennial Park to the safe and cosy surrounds of Durty Nelly's (sponsors of the Michael Cusack's GAA club, incidentally). Our own little Saturday Club would become an ingrained tradition that only the pointy end of the championship could tear us away from.

Every week discussions on team line-ups, how lads had been going in training, the previous week's game and the match ahead the following morning were all on the agenda in our impromptu 'clubhouse'. The logic, we'd convinced ourselves, was that if we had a few pints on the Saturday afternoon we'd be home early and ready to roll on the Sunday morning out in Auburn. You really can convince yourself of anything sometimes. Without the Saturday Club, we reckoned, the weekends would be a washout. Problems only started to creep in when the Saturday Club began morphing into the Sunday Club, too. Still, no better way to spend a Sunday afternoon than sitting in a group of ten people from as far apart as Kilkenny, Waterford, Limerick, Dublin and Offaly picking the team of the '90s or the top ten goalkeepers of the century in order. There was very little time left for the actual hurling. Still, we were enjoying ourselves.

The hurlers in NSW – and the Shamrocks, in particular – were at first glance much more laid-back than their brothers and sisters in the footballing fraternity. To the untrained eye, almost less competitive. Whereas the footballers would spend the back end of the summer months sweating their guts out with physical drills and stamina training to combat the oppressive heat that lay in store, the Shamrocks were content to let the hurling do the talking. A quick warm-up, a bit of a game and then a couple of beers on the side of the field after the warm-down. No worries. It really was paradise to train at Centennial Park. The Sydney Cricket Ground, home of the Sydney Swans, is visible from the sideline and the park is pulsating with life from cricket games to touch rugby leagues. I found myself wondering what the professional footballers across in the SCG would make of the 25 Irish lads with sticks having a cold beer after a light session, as under-7 soccer players were put through their paces nearby. Truth was, the locals hardly batted an eyelid.

SUNDAY, 18 MAY 2008

The league was now coming to a head, and after a draw with the Pat's and a win over the Coast we knew we had Craobh Pádraig to beat to reach a semi-final. My fellow Lucan lads had moved on to Melbourne a few weeks before, but I had decided to stay on in Sydney. I was now the sole Sarsfields man on the panel and was spending most of my time with the Saturday Club. Our squad numbers were beginning to thin out, so it was becoming a case of looking under stones for hurlers. It's funny what you can find under there sometimes, though.

On the way to training the day before the match, I spotted a lad in a Tipperary jersey on the bus with a hurl in his hand and so I waltzed up to say hello. The guy turned out to be a Tipperary man by the name of Richie Fanning and he was on his way to train with Craobh Pádraig, having only just landed in Australia. I began a quick geography of the place, explaining how Pat's actually trained miles away from the bus stop on the other side of the park. No point in going all that way if you haven't signed for them yet, or so the argument went. About 15 minutes later, Richie was pucking around with the rest of the Shamrocks.

With numbers a bit light, Fleece had decided to throw him straight into the mix at full-forward for the next morning's crucial clash. Winner – through to a semi-final. Loser – go home. Fanning would go on to bang in 2–2 from play in our 3–15 to 1–8 win. Not bad for a lad I'd met at a bus stop.

SUNDAY, 25 MAY 2008

It was league semi-final day at long last and with the onset of the knockout stage our heads were now well and truly back in the game. Michael Cusack's had been the front-runners throughout the year and we knew we'd have to produce something special to beat them in a semi-final.

It had been a lean few years on the field for the club and they were hungry for silverware. Founded in 1988, Cusack's are the biggest club in NSW, fielding teams in football, hurling and ladies' football each and every year. They've won all there is to win over the years; however, at the time they were in the midst of a major drought. They weren't used to waiting so long for trophies. A club steeped in tradition, one of their founding fathers is also their most famous son. Clare footballer Seamus Clancy had joined with fellow Claremen Kevin Malone, Aidan McDermott, John Petty, David Fahy and Noel Canavan, as well as Limerick man Eddie McGrath, to set up the club twenty years earlier – a last act from Clancy before returning home in 1989 to lead Clare to their first and only Munster Senior Football Championship three years later. He remains Clare's only All Star footballer. Pedigree.

In 1989, the club set up its hurling team, winning the championship in their first year with a mish-mash of players from Cork, Clare, Waterford, Limerick, Tipperary and Kilkenny. They'd won all there was to win over the course of their long and storied history, but they hadn't tasted success since 2004 at the Central Coast tournament and they wanted it badly in this, their 20th anniversary year as a club. That hunger would show its teeth in the league semi in Auburn, and Cusack's would duly steamroll us before going on to win a thriller against table-toppers Coast in the final the following Sunday: 2–12 to 1–13 after extra-time in one of the games of the year. Cusack's had finally won something and the colour was beginning to come back into their faces. Turned out they were only getting started for 2008.

SATURDAY, 14 JUNE 2008 – MELBOURNE

With the league campaign done and dusted, the GAA in NSW took a brief hiatus before the championship kicked off on 24 June. By some suspicious fluke, the gap between the league's end and the championship's beginning had fallen kindly on the weekend of the Irish rugby Test against the Wallabies in Melbourne. Thousands of Irish had come from all over the country for the game and the city was buzzing with atmosphere. It's not every day you get to see an Irish international side at any code live and in person Down Under, so it tends to become a festival event when it happens. I was certainly relishing the chance to take it all in.

I'd flown down from Sydney the night before to Avalon airport, one of two airports in the Melbourne area. After checking in at the hotel in the city centre, I'd hopped in a cab to meet up with my mates who had been calling Melbourne home for the past few months. They were enjoying a few quiet pints in Bridie O'Reilly's in South Yarra as I rocked in. Apparently, I'd only just missed a few of the Irish team, who had been sent around the Irish pubs on 'meet and greet' duty. Malcolm O'Kelly and Ian Dowling had been behind the bar pulling pints and posing for photographs just minutes before. Dowling, in particular, it seemed, had been relishing his ambassadorial duties. I spotted him back in Sydney a week later full of the joys of spring.

Saturday morning had quickly rolled along and I'd made my plans for the day ahead. Kick-off in the Ireland game wasn't until later that evening, so I had decided to take in an AFL game to pass the afternoon. Luckily, I was staying just around the corner from the spiritual home of Aussie Rules. The Melbourne Cricket Ground (MCG) is the home, officially, of the Melbourne Demons Football Club – the place where Dubliner Jim Stynes built his legacy. Jim had since made Melbourne his permanent home and his entire family, including former Dublin midfielder and brother Brian, had set up shop there, too. Just that week the former Ballyboden St Enda's man had been named as the Demons' new club chairman. From a relatively unknown Dublin minor to a Brownlow Medal winner and AFL club chairman . . . it really was quite the Cinderella story.

I would get hold of Jim a few months later for a chat, but I was in Melbourne that day to see the Western Bulldogs take on the Brisbane Lions. As soon as I had learned of the date for the rugby match I had been looking forward to this game – and in particular the chance to see Laois man Colm Begley in action at first hand. Unfortunately, injury had held Begley back all season and, as Mayo star Pearce Hanley was yet to make his breakthrough in the Brisbane senior side, there was no Irish interest to hand. Either way, it was a tremendously enjoyable experience to see stars such as Jason Akermanis and Adam Cooney (who would go on to win the Brownlow Medal that year) taking on the game's biggest superstar – and highest-paid player – Jonathan Brown. The Bulldogs would duly hammer the Lions in a fairly one-sided encounter, but I had little time to dwell. The Ireland game was due to start three hours later.

The Telstra Dome (which would become Etihad Stadium in March 2009) sits on the opposite side of the city to the MCG. It's primarily used as an Aussie Rules ground (nine of the sixteen teams in the AFL are from Melbourne), but it also gets a run-out for soccer internationals and the odd rugby match. On the way up to the ground, I stopped off at the Celtic Club for a quick look around. I had heard a lot about the place, and by all accounts it's an institution for the Irish population in Victoria. In the absence of any official Irish government presence (the Irish Embassy is in Canberra and the Consul General in Sydney), it offers an unofficial go-to spot for Irish in trouble. It had just recently been refurbished and the new beer garden was packed with Irish jerseys. The atmosphere was building. Swarms of green wigs, Guinness hats and canary yellow Wallaby scarves were flowing towards the Telstra Dome as I joined the wave crossing the Yarra River. Irish hopes were high. The week before, across the Tasman Sea, Ireland had almost caused a sensation by beating the All Blacks. Nearly, as the man says, never won the race, but against what is perceived to be a weaker Wallabies side the fans think they sense an upset in the air.

Eddie O'Sullivan had departed the Irish head coaching job after the disappointment of the World Cup and a disastrous Six Nations, and Michael Bradley was at the helm for the tour Down Under – newly appointed coach Declan Kidney wouldn't take over the reins for a few weeks. On the whole it had been a good tour for Bradley, and for his credentials. But Ireland had failed to reach their own level of expectation once again.

The Australians, with new head coach Robbie Deans pulling the strings, managed to eke out a narrow 18–12 victory. Bradley, and captain Brian O'Driscoll, were clearly disappointed by what had transpired as they sat in the post-match press room reaching for positives. Outside the ground, however, spirits were still high.

It's always party time in Melbourne when there's an Irish team in town. Trying to get a beer in any Irish bar in the city by this stage was absolutely pointless, though. I was running late, and at the time Melbourne had just introduced a citywide curfew, meaning no person could be granted entry to a licensed premises of any description after 2 a.m. Apparently, there'd been some trouble in recent months. Jaded, I decided just to call it a night.

AROUND THE WORLD IN GAA DAYS

SUNDAY, 15 JUNE 2008

After a great night's sleep, I checked out of the hotel and thought about making my way to Gaelic Park in Keysborough, 40 minutes south of the city. The Victoria GAA season was kicking off that morning and I was keen to take a look around the place. The home of the Victoria GAA is renowned as being the best GAA facility in the country. Just like in Sydney, however, the fact that it's so far away from the centre of Melbourne, and the heart of the Irish backpacker community, was proving half its undoing. You really needed a car in these places. Unperturbed by the distance and the cost of getting there (I wasn't sure when I'd be back in Melbourne again), I was off to hail a cab when my phone rang.

My mate Joey had been hurling with the Melbourne Shamrocks club since moving to Victoria some months back and his side had been due to take on Garryowen that day. However, the heavy night before had put paid to the hope of any such fixture going ahead as planned. It was always on the cards. With the plan for the afternoon now washed away in a beery haze, I was veering towards a loose end. Luckily, a Plan B was afoot.

The biggest footy game of the season thus far in Melbourne was due to kick off at 2.10 p.m. My boss, Billy, had managed to rustle up a few tickets, so I decided to go along with my mates Ger and Mark. The place was absolutely buzzing as we got off the tram outside the MCG. The biggest rivalry in the AFL was set to kick off any minute and the place was jam-packed. More than 80,000 had turned up to watch Carlton take on Collingwood.

There was also an Irish element to the game. Marty Clarke had been the sensation of the AFL season in 2007, with a remarkable breakthrough year. He had come to fame as a marauding wing-back – just like Tadhg Kennelly at the Swans – and had been quite unlucky not to win the Rookie of the Year award. After a slow start to the season under head coach Mick Malthouse (who would later manage the Australian International Rules team), Clarke was slowly coming good and rediscovering the kind of form that had seen adoring fans make highlight reels of his best moments on YouTube.

In the Carlton Blues corner, meanwhile, Setanta Ó hAilpín had really been struggling to keep his place in the first team. For the day, thankfully, Blues coach Brett Ratten had given the young Corkman a start at full-back. Setanta, with plenty to prove, meant business.

The stage was set for a humdinger, and one duly emerged. The planets aligned for Setanta as the day progressed and after what was the best first quarter of his AFL career in many people's minds, he came close to being named the Best and Fairest on the pitch (the AFL's version of Man of the Match). Clarke had been quieter, but nonetheless impressive, especially with his ability to kick the bright red egg they call a football. Carlton went on to beat their arch nemesis, however, thanks to a stunning display from superstar and 2006 International Rules villain Brendan Fevola. (Remember the guy who was sent home after a run-in with a barman in Galway?)

The atmosphere was sensational – raw and passionate. It was by far the closest thing I'd seen on my travels to the wilds of a Tipp/Cork Munster final in Thurles, or a Dublin/Meath Leinster decider in Croker. It had left me wanting more. Thankfully, I'd get my wish and would be back at the MCG again before the year was out.

SUNDAY, 24 AUGUST 2008

Things had been quiet in Sydney since the rugby weekend, and the Shamrocks had experienced a championship to forget. Since June we'd beaten Michael Cusack's once and had been given a walkover by the Coast in between defeats to Pat's and Cusack's. Pat's had finished top of the group with Cusack's second, us third and Coast fourth. Two weeks previously we'd beaten a demoralised Coast to book a spot in the semi-finals. Once again, Cusack's were blocking our path to a decider. We knew what the prize was for victory in the semis – a spot in the final against our bitter rivals, Pat's. It was a prize we all really wanted. It just turned out that Cusack's wanted it more.

We had been a shell of a team all winter long and had come nowhere near the heights of Gosford. Players had come and gone and, to be fair, it probably would have been an injustice had we reached the final ahead of a Cusack's team that were the best in the state by far. We duly fell at that second-last hurdle and as a result we were left to watch the final from the sidelines.

Pat's versus league champions Cusack's on a scorcher in Sydney – there are surely worse ways to spend a Sunday afternoon. Cusack's had been strong all year long but seemed to have saved their best for last. In a fairly one-sided final, Newcastle West native Alan O'Connor fired home 1–9 on his own to see Cusack's claim a long overdue championship to add to their league title. There was no begrudging that the best team had won the championship; easy call to make from a sideline when you're not involved. It's unlikely Pat's felt the same way.

The best entertainment for the 500 or so spectators on hand had been put on earlier that day. In a bona fide camogie thriller, Pat's had beaten the Coast by 5–10 to 5–9, while in the ladies' football final Clan na Gael had beaten Cormac McAnallen's by 2–11 to 1–9. The football final was the last to be decided on the main field, as Young Ireland's took on McAnallen's, and this was what the crowds had come to see.

Still stinging from their league final defeat, McAnallen's were unmerciful as they beat Ireland's by 3–7 to 1–5 to claim the first championship in the club's young history. Again, there were very few begrudgers. I was certainly delighted for them. I'd come to know Tyrone natives Liam O'Hara and Eamon Eastwood, the club's founders, quite well over the course of the year. I'd trained with them on a number of occasions and there was certainly no doubting the work these boys had put in. While many of the rest of us were supping beers and taking it handy, these boys had spent dark evenings down in rock pools on Bronte Beach, working on fitness and stamina levels. It was a serious operation. Now, they had finally won some silverware. It might only have been three years old, but the club had a massive future.

McAnallen's put on a massive fundraising banquet a week later in Sydney's Darling Harbour. Tadhg Kennelly, Colm Begley and Tyrone legend Peter Canavan all came along to answer questions on stage as part of the entertainment, hosted and presented by Melbourne AFL writer and Cavan native Catherine Murphy. The club were raising money for a defibrillator for NSW GAA. It's that kind of club.

Before the untimely death of Tyrone star Cormac McAnallen, who passed away unexpectedly in 2004 of an undetected heart condition, the word 'defibrillator' hadn't meant much to most GAA folk, but since Cormac's death it had become a necessary requirement for all sporting groups back home, particularly in the GAA world. NSW were just catching up. Heart conditions, as we're all aware, know no borders.

Coincidentally, Michael Cusack's also had their 20th anniversary banquet the following week and welcomed players past and present to a gala night in the city.

The GAA season in NSW was ending on a high. I had been really looking forward to attending both, but unfortunately I had a book to finish.

Next stop: Auckland.

10

THE LAND OF THE
LONG WHITE CLOUD

WEDNESDAY, 27 AUGUST 2008 – AUCKLAND

It had been almost a full year since I'd set out from Dublin on my little lap of the world and by now the travel bug was back in earnest. I was looking forward to the three weeks I had ahead of me, with Auckland, San Francisco, Chicago, New York and Dublin all pencilled in on the itinerary. It seemed a daunting task, but after the ground I'd managed to cover over the course of the past year I was confident I could do it. My friends Joey and Mark were starting their own little adventure around New Zealand at the same time and were there to meet me in the YHA hostel in Auckland when I landed. It was nice to think that there would be some friendly faces around, even if just for a day. Of course, we ended up straight out on the beer.

Our first stop was the infamous Father Ted's, which sits just off the main city thoroughfare of Queen Street. Joey and Mark only had one night in Auckland and were due to head off on a bus tour around the country the following morning, so we set about making the most of it. By 8 a.m. the next day, with pounding heads, the lads had packed up and headed off on their travels. I, on the other hand, had other business to attend to.

My first task was to get my bearings: where was I and where was I going? A local sightseeing tour seemed like just the plan. Amazingly, I was the only person on the bus and so a kind of personal tour evolved from there. The driver showed me the harbour, the Auckland Sky Tower and all the rest of the sights in the city. From the top of the tower, the views were breathtaking. And it was unseasonably warm and sunny at the time. One thing really struck me, though: the city had the exact same layout as Sydney. I'm sure there's some reason for that, but I never found out what it was. Either way, it made me feel right at home.

With only a few days left, I planned to meet Auckland GAA president Liam O'Keeffe in Father Ted's bar the next night. I'd been in touch with my original Auckland contact, Gerald Lohan, only to discover that he'd since moved on to Fiji. He'd passed on O'Keeffe's contact details but had also taken the time to tell me of his plans to 'convert this rugby-mad nation to Gaelic games', as he'd put it. No better man. Lohan had been the secretary of the Auckland GAA for the previous two years and had seen some great things and heard some great stories in his time, featuring characters such as Vincent McHale from Mayo, who had lived in Auckland for 50 years after becoming the first St Jarlath's Hogan Cup-winning captain, and All Black legend and local GAA star ZinZan Brooke.

The place definitely had a story to tell.

THURSDAY, 28 AUGUST 2008

Sitting in the corner of Father Ted's at 8 p.m., I saw Liam O'Keeffe walk into the pub. I hadn't come across any other Irish bars in my few days in Auckland and assumed Father Ted's to be the principal haunt. It was certainly the only one I'd heard of before landing in New Zealand. After a quick beer and a brief chat, Liam suggested we head over to the real local. Sounded like quite the plan in my book, and after about 15 minutes in the car we arrived at the Clare Inn in Mount Eden.

Mount Eden is where the majority of the Irish population call home, and the GAA playing pitches are just around the corner at a place called Seddon Fields. Eden Park, the home of the Auckland

Blues Super 14 rugby team, lies just across the road, but as I walked through the door of the Clare Inn I was pleasantly surprised to be greeted by what felt like the closest thing to a bar from home that I'd come across in the past 12 months. The only other place to come close was the Welcome Hotel in Sydney. Both pubs are run by Clare men – Lar Collins at the Welcome and Noel Quinlivan at the Clare. Surely that can't be a coincidence.

The atmosphere in the Clare was warm and welcoming, and I was soon introduced to a few of the lads from the GAA committee, Mick O'Malley, a long-time New Zealand GAA man who is originally from west Belfast but has lived there for over 35 years, and the new secretary of the Auckland GAA, 21-year-old Roscommon native Kevin McGarry. McGarry had come to New Zealand to take up work on a farm in Hamilton. In August 2007, he had been involved in a horrific accident and had lost both of his legs, also suffering serious burns to half his body. It had all happened one morning at around 4.30 a.m., when he had gone out to bring in the cows. The Suzuki 125cc on which he had been travelling got caught in a ditch and flipped, leaving the Kilnamanagh man trapped under both his bike and an electric fence. Before he could struggle his way free, petrol had begun to spill from the bike. He doesn't remember much after that. He drifted in and out of consciousness for about half an hour before being found, but he told me he does remember looking down and seeing his charred legs.

McGarry had been released from hospital in March 2008 and was beginning to find his way again through his involvement in the GAA and the local soccer club. Efforts had been ongoing ever since the accident to raise the NZ$160,000 necessary for the prosthetic legs Kevin was after. He had vowed not to return to Ireland until he could walk from the plane himself. His courage and good humour are quite literally an inspiration, even to a cynical, moany old hack like myself. There's a lot we can learn.

Unfortunately, McGarry and O'Malley were on their way out the door as I arrived, but we agreed to meet the following day at the Clare for a proper chat. Liam and I hung on for a few more beers, but I soon called it a night and headed home to pack. After I met up with the lads the next afternoon, I was straight off to the airport for a flight to San Francisco.

FRIDAY, 29 AUGUST 2008

I landed at the Clare Inn around noon and went straight for the Irish brekkie, as I waited for the lads to arrive. I was nervous about the flight ahead. It's a serious head-spinner. After twelve hours in the air, I'd touch down in California three hours before I took off in Auckland. That's the international dateline for you. I was still trying to get my head around it when Kevin and Mick arrived in the door.

We weren't long in settling into a few pints – it was Friday afternoon, after all – and soon got to chatting about the local GAA scene. Mick has seen a lot in his time in Auckland and quickly ran me through some of the highlights. Outside of his distinguished years on the field as a player, O'Malley, alongside fellow coaches Rocky Conway and Malachy McAfee, had the distinction of leading Auckland to their first-ever Australasian State Games senior football title back in 1992. It had taken extra-time before captain Paddy McCahill had lifted the trophy after an epic final – a definite high-point in the history of the GAA there.

I'd heard so much about the legend Rocky Conway even before landing in New Zealand. He had played under Eamon Coleman on the famous 1983 Derry All-Ireland Minor Football Championship-winning team and my mate Aidan Glover, who'd once called Auckland home, had told me all about him before I'd left. I was gutted, however, to discover that he happened to be back in Ireland while I was there.

There were certainly plenty of other interesting characters to keep me occupied, though. The legacy of Gaelic games in Auckland is quite the colourful one. Bagnelstown man Paddy Somers had given a brief insight into the early days of the GAA on the North Island on the association website a few years previously. According to him, Gaelic games in Auckland could be traced back as far as 1949. A provincial Feis had been held the following year in which Auckland, Wellington and Christchurch had all fielded teams, and from there the GAA scene had begun to take shape. The really interesting development had happened in the 1960s.

A priest named Father Leo Doyle had begun a programme to introduce the local kids to Gaelic games through the formation of a Junior Football Board. Young players from all over the city were drawn in to take part in the games, primarily through the Catholic schools and most notably through the Marist Brothers. Such foresight would secure the future of the association in Auckland for a very long time and in 1989 it would reap its first major reward, when the minors of Auckland would win the Australasian State title. It would most certainly not be their last, either. From such small acorns had the GAA grown here, and such initiatives had led to many famous faces wearing the colours of the Auckland GAA, and particularly those of the Rangers club. The 1987 World Cup-winning All Black rugby union star Bernie McCahill (whose parents hail from Donegal) and the infamous back-row forward ZinZan Brooke, who has no Irish background to speak of but who embraced the game of Gaelic football with incredible vigour, are probably the two best examples. GAA men to the core, apparently.

People of this calibre have been coming through the system in New Zealand regularly because of the commitment of the people that believe in it and who have dedicated a large portion of their lives towards it. People such as Jimmy Connolly from Connemara, for example, who has trained seven successful Auckland All-Australasian Minor Football Championship-winning teams. Every player on every one of those teams was native Kiwi. Quite simply amazing, if you think about it.

I was heartened to hear how the GAA has gone from strength to strength in Auckland and was delighted to have met some of the people responsible for that. On another level, however, I was beginning to notice an increasingly worrying trend. How was it that places with relatively tiny Irish populations such as

Singapore, Auckland and even Adelaide could have so much success at underage level in bringing local kids on board, yet areas with huge Irish populations like Sydney continued to struggle? New South Wales wasn't even able to put together a minor team for the State Games a few months later. Auckland wouldn't be travelling to those Games either, O'Keeffe told me. Apparently, the cost of flying to South Australia was just too much for them to pull a team together. Wellington/Hutt Valley, from the south of the North Island, would be the only New Zealand representative at those championships in October.

For now, I had to say my farewells and head for the airport. It was actually a painful task to tear myself away from the place, but I was already running ridiculously late. My flight was due to leave in two hours and it was 4 p.m. on a Friday evening. I had completely lost track of time talking to the lads, but luckily a friend of theirs, Sean Cullen, had popped in for a quick pint after work. He offered to drop me at the airport, and in fairness it was an absolute lifesaver. Unfortunately, it was too late to squeeze in a flying visit to Ger Lohan in Fiji. Pity.

Either way, I had little to regret. It's onwards and upwards to the good old US of A.

NORTH AMERICA

11

TREASURE ISLAND

A 17-hour time difference (it was actually the next day, as far as the body clock was concerned) combined with a 12-hour flight and the rigours of US immigration had served to make for a rocky start to my time in San Francisco. I was struggling to find my bearings. Even the seasons had changed from southern to northern hemisphere. It was summertime in the Bay Area of California and the sun was splitting the stones.

It was quickly back to the old reliable, as I set about gaining a foothold in my surroundings. The simplest solution is often the most effective and so I headed for the first Irish bar I could find, hoping to come across an Irishman for a heads-up. Works almost every time.

The first Irish watering hole to land in the crosshairs in San Fran was the Irish Bank. It used to be called the Bank of Ireland, but seemingly someone in a Dublin office had taken umbrage to the use of the name and legal proceedings had ensued. Water under the bridge, but an interesting sidenote nonetheless. Inside the door just two minutes and a familiar face soon came into view – Conor O'Neill, a friend of mine from my college days in Maynooth and a former barman at my local bar there, the Roost. Conor had been working in San Fran for a year and it turned out that his older brother, Ronan, actually owned the place.

It was a nice little bar, with genuine sporting memorabilia adorning the walls. It was still frequented largely by Americans, though, just like most downtown San Francisco bars, apart from Foley's just around the corner, I was told. One piece of sporting memorabilia caught my eye almost immediately – a flag from Scottish golf course Carnoustie, alongside the big smiley head of Padraig Harrington. Apparently, the now three-time Major winner had ventured up from southern California to say hello to Ronan after winning a particularly lucrative tournament run by a certain Tiger fellow a few years before. O'Neill, Padraig's caddy Ronan Flood and a few others had embarked upon a celebratory pub crawl around the city that night with a million-dollar cheque in the back seat of the car. Harrington was the designated driver. Now pictures of the twice British Open champion and his Claret Jug sit proudly in collage form on the wall of the Irish Bank. There's no sign of Padraig returning any time soon, but Ronan Flood's brother was about to land in town. You sensed a heavy session could be in the offing.

Time was somewhat short for me, and after being taken on a pub crawl of my own by the two O'Neill boys I decided that discretion was the better part of valour and tucked myself away in the hotel for a few hours' kip. I still wasn't quite sure what day it was. The time difference was bloody murder.

SATURDAY, 30 AUGUST 2008

The O'Neill boys had given me a great insight into the atmosphere and spirit of the city the night before. Perhaps too many spirits. My head was absolutely pounding as I headed for breakfast. Geographically, I was still a little hazy, so I booked myself a sightseeing bus tour. After six hours or so on the thankfully air-conditioned bus, I now knew which bridge is which, which way is north and how many thousands of movies had been filmed in the place. The only thing I'd known beforehand was just how many thousands of miles Kilkenny City was from the Irish Bank (thanks to a particularly helpful signpost hanging on the outside wall of Ronan's pub). Tours are great, but it's only the locals who can really show you how everyday life is in any given place. They tend not to live in the vicinity of the run-down backpacker hostels, unsurprisingly enough.

San Francisco is undeniably Irish in both obvious and understated ways. Street names and Irish bars are usually a giveaway to some form of Irish influence, but the size and scale of the Irish community there, just like anywhere else in the world, can often best be judged by the GAA barometer. In San Francisco, it was about to burst its top. It's hardly surprising that the association there is massive. It is the United States, after all. However, unless you've been to the Treasure Island GAA grounds – on a man-made oasis halfway between San Francisco and Oakland – you've never seen ambition on such a scale. It's probably the biggest individual project outside of Ireland undertaken in the last ten years: the new home of the San Francisco GAA. The next morning I was to be shown around the place.

SUNDAY, 31 AUGUST 2008

It was early on the Sunday morning as Corkman John O'Flynn pulled up outside Johnny Foley's bar on the aptly named O'Farrell Street. He'd just come from watching yet another heartbreaking All-Ireland series loss to Kerry for his native county at the Irish Culture Centre in the west of the city, the area in which most of the settled Irish community live. The Kerry/Cork situation was getting tiresome. How many times do you have to beat the Kingdom, exactly? Believe it or not, the last team other than Kerry to beat Cork in a senior football championship match was Fermanagh back in the 2004 qualifiers. I'd be getting sick of it too, if I were a Corkman. O'Flynn had family over from Ireland at the time and on the way out to the site of the new home of the GAA he stopped off to pick them up from his house. I was brought inside the place and offered smoked salmon sandwiches and a cup of Barry's Tea. Just what the doctor ordered. It was a beautiful morning as we set off across the city.

AROUND THE WORLD IN GAA DAYS

Treasure Island is an incredibly ambitious project and, when I set eyes upon it for the first time, I was utterly stunned by its scale. O'Flynn was able to run me through the ins and outs of every blade of grass and every pour of concrete as we walked around the yet-to-be-seeded fields. I was wondering how the Corkman had the time to do anything else. While he had been heavily involved in the Treasure Island development, outside of his role with the San Francisco GAA he was also the co-chairman of the Continental Youth Championships (CYC) programme in the San Francisco area and the co-chairman of the CYC for the entire North American County Board (NACB).

John's children, nieces and nephews were running around freely as he ran the adults through the plans for the next stage of the Treasure Island development. Time was of the essence, with the All Stars football tour due to land there in December. It would be more than just a jewel in the crown when the touring players took the field; it would be something special.

Melbourne, Chicago and Boston have probably the three best sets of GAA facilities outside Europe. They all have wonderful fields and dressing-rooms that a lot of people have worked very hard to secure. The main drawback to these grounds, however – Gaelic Park, Keysborough and Canton, in Chicago, Melbourne and Boston respectively – is that they all lie roughly an hour or so from where most of the local Irish populations live. Considering the transient nature of a lot of young Irish men and women who pass through these places, such a distant location can often be problematic. Potential players can so easily come and go without ever having any dealings with the local GAA. This wouldn't be a problem for San Francisco. Not after this year. Seven minutes on a bus from downtown and you're pitchside at the Treasure Island fields. All four or so of them.

Back in March 2008 the GAA began work on one of the most ambitious projects in international GAA history. Once completed there would be up to four full-size fields going at the one time, with as many as twelve juvenile fields ready to rock, depending on the event in question. The largest undertaking for San Fran's new home would be the 2009 Continental Youth Championships. The CYCs are a massive event each year in North America and the organisation required to host them is quite simply mind-boggling. But judging by what I'd seen at Treasure Island, it would be like a walk in the park to people of the ilk of O'Flynn. With hundreds of young American kids running wild at the CYCs, it would be quite the sight to behold, at any rate.

The seeding of the grass on the playing fields was due to begin in the next week or so. One smaller juvenile field sits up the front of the site beside the largely Irish-run rugby club from whence the idea originally came, but back at the other end of the island, about two blocks down, sits yet another juvenile field and two full-size pitches the size of two Croke Parks. It was really hard to fathom the scale of this project. After weeks of digging and processing the concrete foundations of what was once a jail, the fields would someday very soon emerge in radiant green when the grass began to peep its head above the topsoil. The project was running right on time, too. The finer details of long-term ownership and such hadn't been nailed down quite yet, but the most important elements certainly had been and the project was nearing completion. There was a big target looming on the horizon in December with the All Stars coming to town.

When GAA president Nickey Brennan and the GAA's overseas development officer, Sheamus Howlin, landed there along with the stars of the 2007 and 2008 football seasons, one knew they'd be more than blown away by what they saw. And not just by the grass. Outside of the main grandstand that is to be erected, the site sits next to a YMCA and the Boys and Girls Club of America (an after-school project keeping underprivileged kids occupied), with whom O'Flynn has been working closely. One of the many schemes worked on by himself and full-time games development administrator Paul Bayly from Louth is to bring local kids on board to play Gaelic games. It has been remarkably successful so far. Having the home of the local GAA in all its new-found splendour right next door can only help further.

The land came with more than just the space on which to build a field. This was a place in which to build a home. Many of the buildings that surround the field development are now the GAA's to do with as they wish. Within their confines are ready-made built-in kitchens, old laundry facilities and 10,000 square feet either side of the main field on which to expand. On one side there will be dressing-rooms, while on the other a clubhouse that will face diagonally out onto the field. The continuing relationship with the YMCA also means that the GAA have access to their existing facilities out there, namely a fully kitted-out gym, a full weights room and a massive hall with four basketball courts, which is currently being used for underage hurling in the winter months. Oh yeah, and handball alleys were coming soon, too. It was hard to even think of a comparable facility in Ireland. No handouts either – this was a real community project from whose example a lot of clubs could learn. All that was left to do now was to name it. Personally, I thought they were onto a winner with Treasure Island.

By the end of my day in the bay, I was just blown away by the whole thing. I was feeling genuinely privileged to have seen the project in its formative stage. It would certainly make for a nice sensation when I watched Nickey Brennan officially open the place on the RTÉ website alongside GAA director general Paraic Duffy that December at the All Stars game. Eventually, they would settle on Páirc na nGael as a title.

I'm eternally grateful to John for taking the time to show me around – he gave me a more comprehensive tour of the whole ground than I could ever have expected. The sun was beginning to dip its head in the sky as John dropped me off back in the city. I grabbed a quick bite to eat, then pulled out my map again. I was due to meet the San Francisco GAA public relations officer at his house in the west of the city a few hours later.

* * *

Limerick man Liam Reidy had been one of those to the fore on the Treasure Island project, in particular through his role in pitching the project to the head honchos in Croke Park. A few weeks before I met him, Liam had been in Croker trying to explain the ins and outs of the whole plan. He even went as far as to go up in a helicopter over the bay and film the site from all sides. He then put together a DVD and presented it to a gobsmacked boardroom at headquarters. The facility wasn't just on a massive scale, it was also in a location anyone would wet themselves for. Footage of the work O'Flynn and Bayly had been doing with the local kids had been thrown into the mix on the DVD, too. At a time when integration was of such importance to the continued success of the association back home, a Limerick man who lived a 12-hour flight away had landed in Dublin with footage of 20-odd African American kids soloing up and down a field on the west coast of the United States. The lads in Croker knew these boys meant business.

Reidy is probably one of the most meticulous and dedicated PROs in the world, considering the vigour with which he approaches his role. A 34 year old, originally from Broadford in West Limerick, he first came to the west coast back in 1997. Outside of the usual weekly grind of organising fundraising projects and the like, he writes all the GAA stuff for the local Irish paper here, a free monthly called the *Irish Herald*. Not just the match reports that you tend to see in a lot of places, but in-depth interviews with lads who played in San Francisco as far back as 60 years ago. He's developed a massive interest in the history of the GAA there, and he runs through the contents of a box of memorabilia with me that he has in his living room. In it he has the entire history of the local association, from old match reports to restored photographs. If anyone's going to write a history of the GAA in San Francisco, I really hope it's this guy.

His most recent project had been a supplement for the local newspaper explaining all about the Treasure Island project. The importance of such a PR exercise can never be overestimated and in real terms the sixteen-page pullout had raised almost five figures for the project. Within its pages, Reidy had compiled comments from people such as former GAA president Joe McDonagh of Galway, Nickey Brennan and Sheamus Howlin. McDonagh even appeared on the DVD.

The pullout also contained all the details of how the lease for Treasure Island had been signed with the City and County of San Francisco back in 2007, while Reidy also made sure to mention the hard work of people such as Pat Uniacke, Mike Darcy, Leo Cassidy and Tom Hunt. It had been a serious team effort and I was genuinely delighted to see what they had achieved. It's amazing how productive the GAA can be when not being choked by its own internal politics. And it is forward-looking and hard-working people such as Reidy who make these things happen. The Limerick man, in fact, had a story to tell on its own merits.

He first came to America in 1995, when he set up shop in New York. There he had hurled with the Limerick club and had won a senior championship straight off the bat. He put that win down mostly to the influence of his teammates that year – Tipperary's Tommy Dunne and Galway's Joe Rabbitte. Probably hard not to. He had enjoyed a day to remember himself in that game, too. He was marking Anthony Daly just two weeks after the Clare captain had lifted the Liam McCarthy Cup. Reidy had plundered a goal off him. Can't but be happy with that.

That wasn't the only illustrious company he had been keeping back in those days, though. After a spell back in Ireland, training and working as a teacher, he came back to the States only to win a North American championship – once again at his first attempt. That particular year it had been another Premier County/ Tribesmen twosome that had helped steer Reidy's team to victory – Tipperary's Declan Carr and Murty Killeagh of Carnmore in Galway. He rates Carr as probably the most successful player ever to hurl in North America. Carr is the only man he knows of who's won the big five – the New York, Boston, Chicago, San Francisco and North American Senior Hurling Championships. Throw in two All-Ireland medals (one as captain in 1991), three All Stars awards, five Munster titles and a National Hurling League to the mix and it would seem Carr certainly hadn't had a bad old career. He would finish it with my club, Lucan Sarsfields. As would his brother, Tommy. Small aul world.

Reidy, who is just completing a PhD in environmental science at Berkeley University, also runs the local GAA website. As we were chatting, he was putting up the scores from the North American championship finals, which had been held earlier that day in Boston. San Francisco had enjoyed success in the junior A football championship through the Ulster club, the Shamrocks had won the junior camogie title, while the Fog City Harps had secured the honours in the intermediate ladies' football championship. Not a bad haul. But it wasn't just teams from San Francisco that were representing the west coast in Massachusetts that weekend.

The scale of the GAA on the west coast of the States is somewhat limited when compared to the scale of the operation on the Eastern Seaboard, but there are still a massive number of clubs in California and its surrounds. The San Francisco area is classified under the Western Division of the NACB and encapsulates the San Francisco, San Jose, Oakland, Burlingame and Bay Area suburbs. There are 14 clubs in San Francisco alone – Cailíní Saoirse, Celts, Clan na Gael, Fog City Harps, Michael Cusack's, Na Fianna, Naomh Pádraig, Sarsfields, Séan Treacy's, Shamrocks, Shannon Rangers, Sons of Ború, Ulster and Young Irelanders. It's only when you take a step back and look at the two other boards on the west coast that you begin to see how widespread the games really are, though. The Southwest Division Board looks after eight clubs from five states – Albuquerque football and hurling in New Mexico, Na Fianna and Setanta (San Diego) and Orange County Róisín and Wild Geese (LA) in California, Denver Gaels in Colorado, Phoenix Gaels in Arizona and the rather colourfully christened Celtic Cowboys in Texas. The Northwest Board, meanwhile, covers two clubs in Washington (Seattle Gaels and Spokane Gaels) and one in Oregon (the Columbia Red Branch in Portland).

Austin had been the big breakthrough artists this year and had managed to bring the first-ever North American County Board championship back to the city from Boston in the form of the Junior D football title. That's where it starts.

Chicago, however, had been the big winners, with four of the major honours winging their way back to Lake Michigan. The Limerick club had won the senior hurling title, St Mary's had secured the senior camogie, the Patriots had beaten Boston Celtics in the Junior C men's football decider, while the McBride's club had seen off Detroit St Ann's in the Junior B ladies' football final.

I was excited. The capital of Illinois, and the home state of Barack Obama, was my next port of call. All roads led to Chi Town.

12

THE WINDY CITY

The jetlag had only just begun to ease its hooks as I landed in Chicago. It hadn't been a particularly long flight, but it was my third plane ride and time zone change in the space of a week, so I was starting to feel the pinch. I had landed at around 7 p.m. and was pleasantly surprised at the lack of invasive scans and searches at the airport.

O'Hare International is pretty big as airports go, but it's also serviced by a pretty regular train service to the city. Unfortunately, it takes about an hour to get to central Chicago from there. I was tired and restless as I boarded the carriage, and an hour later I was boarding another one to take me on to the hostel I had booked in San Francisco. I'd only got the bones of two days there and the pressure was really on.

When I had set out from Ireland almost a year earlier, I had planned to feature Chicago quite heavily in the book, but time, money and circumstances had conspired to force me into a flying visit. But I couldn't very well write a book about the GAA outside Europe and not mention the Windy City.

I hadn't got a whole lot organised at that point, but was keen to settle in and get a good night's sleep before I set about trying to find my way around. Luckily, I was completely wrecked as I reached the hostel. Too wrecked even to take full stock of my surrounds. I wouldn't have let a dog lie down in that place.

TUESDAY, 2 SEPTEMBER 2008

A lack of air conditioning in the 35-degree heat made for a somewhat uncomfortable night's rest. The eight-bed dorm was serviced by three roaring plug-in fans and populated by a gang of six travelling Dublin teenagers, though they had landed in from a night on the tiles at around 8 a.m. as I was heading out the door.

The train from near Lafayette University on the Northside where I was staying is pretty regular and I happily escaped the hostel to join the masses en route to work. Chicago is renowned as being one of the sporting capitals of the United States and a quick scour through the pages of the *Chicago Sun-Times* quickly confirmed what I'd suspected – the place was sports mad, and it was play-off season. Both the White Sox (Southside) and Cubs (Northside) baseball teams had been well in the hunt for the knockout stages of the Major League Baseball competition and excitement was fever pitch on both sides of the city. As I was reading through the doomsayer columnists' views on the Cubs' hopes of actually winning their first World Series since 1908 (they reckon they've been cursed ever since), the train sailed past the storied Wrigley Field. I had duly taken note. Luckily, the Cubbies were in town and I certainly couldn't very well come to Chi Town for a few days and not take in a game. For the time being, though, I was still just trying to find my way around.

A bus tour was first on the agenda, and I was quick to realise that it is a pretty big place. The heat was oppressive. I was still trying to adjust, coming from the Aussie winter. Thankfully, it's easier to get used to the heat than it is to adapt to the cold. It gets to below freezing there in the winter, but it was midsummer, so I'd little to be moaning about.

I was shown around all the sights on the little tour – the Hancock Building, the Opera House and out around Navy Pier. The pier is one of the biggest tourist attractions in the city and originally housed the world's first Ferris wheel, which had been erected for the first World's Fair in 1893. It's gone now, but I am taken aback by the tour guide's insistence that Lake Michigan, on which the city sits, is actually the world's largest supply of freshwater. Feck the oil, this is where you wanna be if it all goes belly up.

The biggest point of interest for me, though, is Soldier Field, home of the resident Chicago NFL team, the Bears, the go-to side when the Cubs and White Sox have called it a day for winter. It's quite a bizarre spectacle. The stadium has just been refurbished, but instead of knocking it down and rebuilding it from scratch, the old stadium has been kept and the new one built around it. It looks like a giant spaceship built around ancient ruins. The Bears' season was due to kick off a few days later, when they would travel to Indianapolis to take on the Colts, and their first home game at Soldier Field wasn't until 21 September against Tampa. I was ruing the fact I was going to miss it. Not that I would have had the slightest hope of getting a ticket anyway.

After a long day's gallivanting around the city, I headed back for the train and onwards to Wrigley. The Cubs had been top of their division for the past few months and looked certain of qualifying for the play-offs. But they were beginning to slip, and nerves on the Northside were frayed. That night the Houston Astros were in town. I rocked up to the stadium and surprisingly secured a ticket pretty handily – the Cubs' slide into mediocrity would continue with another devastating loss, as I sat in the stands. Pretty depressing stuff, to be honest.

The experience nonetheless had been worthwhile for me. I'd always wanted to see the famous stadium and the ivy that drapes its outfield walls at the bleachers. It's quite a unique setting in many ways. Throngs of bars surround the ground, but three or four are higher than the outer walls of the stadium and for a few extra bucks you can sit on the roof of one of them and take in the game from there. It's always party time in the bleachers at Wrigley. The people love their baseball above all else. Even if they have been starved of success for over 100 years. On the Northside, anyway.

After the game I headed for the exit, but the queue for the train back home was long, so I decided to stop off for a quick pint. I walked south from the ground until I came across a bar called the Blarney Stone. It's all very American around there (unsurprisingly enough) and I got the impression I was unlikely to come across an Irish barman despite the abundance of Irish bars. I fancied a beer all the same, though, and with no ID on me I reckoned the Blarney Stone might be the only place I'd get one. The drinking age is 21 and most bars are ridiculously strict on it – it's not uncommon to see middle-aged men with grey beards being ID'd at the door. The only identification I had with me was my passport and that never left the bag when I knew there was going to be beer involved. The frightening thought of losing the damn thing just wasn't worth the hassle. And so I was keen to find a sympathetic ear that might recognise the Irish accent. I duly wandered through the door of the Blarney Stone and waltzed up to the bar and grabbed a seat. Lo and behold, the lad serving me was Irish.

Kieren Fahy had called Chicago home for a number of years and he tells me that he used to play a fair bit of GAA in his day. These days, however, his time is taken up with work. He was a real estate agent for a company called Sussex and Reilly at the time, but also did some shifts at the Blarney Stone every now and then. I would later learn that he'd been quite the useful footballer back in the day with his club at home in Ardrahan, Co. Galway, but he'd lost touch with a lot of the lads in the GAA out in the US. He steered me in the right direction, towards a few other local bars that might be able to offer some insight. I headed for home and prepared for another day, my last in the Windy City.

WEDNESDAY, 3 SEPTEMBER 2008

Heading back in the direction of Wrigley Field, I sought out the first spot Kieren had suggested. The Irish Oak bar sits on North Clarke Street and was completely deserted on the Wednesday morning I walked in the door. I was happily tucking into a full Irish breakfast (you just can't get a decent bit of a sausage back in Australia, so I was happy to take them while I could) as Billy Lawless walked in the door. Lawless has called Chicago home for a very long time now and knows all the lads in the local GAA, past and present. He knows enough to be able to confirm what I'd already feared – that the entire GAA population of Illinois was still in Boston at the NACB championships. Either that, or those who had returned were still in bed recovering. The conversation moved on as I told him about my little project. He pricked his ears as I went through my experiences in Dubai. Turned out the Galway man running the Burj Al Arab hotel was actually Billy's brother. Honest to God.

Unfortunately, Billy couldn't stay long to chat, as he was off to a meeting. Outside of the Irish Oak, and the several other projects around the city he's also heavily involved in, he is a central part of the Celts for Immigration Reform movement, which was founded back in 2006. The US had become a different place since 9/11. Having been here both before and after the September 2001 attacks, I can certainly see the difference. It's hard not to at the airports. On the ground, however, it was the fear- and war-mongering that were having a far more serious and life-changing effect on the illegal Irish population. The Bush government's Patriot Act had done more than just shore up the country's borders. It had also made life here for illegal immigrants a living nightmare. In years gone by, in Chicago as in Boston and New York, Irish illegals had flown largely under the radar. They had kept themselves to themselves and gone on to contribute hugely to the national economy – indeed, to the national culture – through business ventures and community activism amongst other things. Now all that was being threatened. The meeting Billy was off to attend was with the Mexican equivalent of the Irish lobby group. The two had been working together to draw attention to the worsening plight of the illegal immigrant in the US. Under the letter of the law (which was now being more stringently enforced than ever before), illegal immigrants could no longer renew their driver's licences without first providing a social security number, and illegal immigrants don't have social security numbers.

A situation was arising whereby Irish people who had called the US home for years could no longer go about their daily business without the fear of God in the backs of their minds. Every time you took to the road under the current climate, you were effectively risking deportation – or worse (under a proposed bill that Lawless's group had been fighting), a year's detention. Deportation from America is pretty much the scariest thing for an illegal who has built a life there, especially if he or she has built a business and secured a home. If you get that tap on the shoulder, it's goodnight and good luck, with just the shirt on your back and the Irish passport in your pocket. Many people weren't willing to risk losing everything they'd worked for over the years and so were now selling up and heading for home while they could still do it of their own volition. Jump before being pushed.

It was election time in the US at the time and the battle between Republican candidate John McCain and his Democratic rival Barack Obama had started to heat up. Rallies were going off everywhere and everyone wanted to have their say. I hadn't thought to question one assumption in all that, though. Surely the Irish were shouting for Obama, right? Nope. Not the lads I'd come across, anyway. Many Irish people, especially the illegals, were rooting for McCain. Apparently, Obama had been slow to address the immigration issue with any real vigour. McCain, on the other hand, had made direct promises and was a darling of the Irish community, particularly in New York, where newspaper man Niall O'Dowd's Irish Lobby for Immigration Reform had its base. It was hard to believe what I was hearing. There, in an Irish bar in the shadows of Wrigley Field, in Obama's home state of Illinois, I was being told that the Irish were shouting for the Republicans. The Republicans who had caused this mess in the first place. Some wonders never cease. It would matter little in the end.

I thank Billy for his time and his insight, and head off back in the direction of the city. My next port of call was the Fadó bar (or at least the Chicago franchise of the nationwide chain), which is run by a Limerick man named Kieran Aherne. He was up to his eyeballs as I walked in the door, but he took a few minutes out for a bit of a chat. He'd been in the States for a long time and actually started off managing a friend's bar in Florida. Now, he'd settled in Chicago as the general manager of Fadó. He'd seen a lot in his time there. We got to chatting about the nature of emigrant life and we duly noted one startling reality – there was hardly a place left on God's green earth where an Irishman could go and not be found. Case in point, Aherne told me a story from a few months previously.

A young Limerick man had left home and hadn't been heard of for over a year. He hadn't been in touch with his family and they had no way to track him down. For a good few days, they had been desperately trying to get word to him of his father's death back home. They had no idea where in the US he might be, but he had last been sighted in the Chicago area. The family had decided to call Fadó, as a family friend known to Aherne had heard that he was working there. Bit of a long-shot. Irish expats being Irish expats, sure enough, Kieran knew the lad in question. He had only been sitting at the bar an hour before the phone call came through. Aherne duly passed the word along.

In some ways, it's comforting to know you can always be found. In other ways, it's frightening to think that you can never really escape. Especially not in America. And especially not as long as you're drinking in Irish bars.

Things were beginning to get a bit hectic in Fadó as the after-work crowd began to swarm the place. Kieran was under pressure, so I decided to take my leave of his company and headed off to my final port of call. Lawless had invited me for dinner that night at the Gage, his restaurant in the city, which he ran with the family. I fully intended to take up his offer at the time, but that was before I landed in the Kerryman. Sitting in the shadow of the Hard Rock Café, it lies just across the road from Fadó and is really quite a lovely spot. I hadn't been sure quite what to expect when I landed but had been very impressed at what I'd found inside its doors. I'd been told that two lads from Kerry in their 20s owned the place and had run it with tremendous success for the past number of years. I pulled up a seat at the bar and within a few minutes Trevor O'Donoghue had popped his head out from a meeting.

The Castleisland native and his twin brother, Michael, had turned an old, abandoned speakeasy into one of the city's most popular and trendy bars. All the cool kids went there, apparently. The lads recalled one particular incident that had stuck in the memory. Back in May, the bar had been packed to the rafters with Munster rugby fans ahead of the Heineken Cup final. The twins had been running around like blue-arsed flies trying to keep everything in order when one of their employees approached them with a problem. Hollywood movie star Johnny Depp was at the door and looking for a table. Of course, there was barely room in the place to swing a cat. The lads took action and set up a tiny table in the far corner up the back. A few stools and a bit of a table. Take it or leave it, boyo. Munster are playing.

Rave reviews of the bar's food and atmosphere line the walls and I soon spotted a fundraising poster for local Gaelic football club St Brendan's. Trevor and Mick still line out regularly for the club's junior team, it turned out, and they also sponsored the squad. Their bar had been themed after the same Brendan – the saint, navigator and Kerryman, who many believe had originally discovered America in his little boat hundreds of years before. The club, of course, had come before the bar, having been set up in 1950. They certainly made fine bedfellows, all the same.

St Brendan's have had many famous sons come through their ranks over the years – most notably former Kildare senior football star Niall Buckley. One of the oldest and most storied clubs in Chicago, Brendan's had, amongst other distinctions, become the first team to play a game at Gaelic Park when it was first opened back in 1984. They have a great little club. In fact, I'd ended up out for half the night with Trevor, Mick and the guts of the St Brendan's senior team.

A lot has changed since Gaelic Park first opened its gates, but on the whole the GAA there has been going strong ever since. Nowadays, Chicago has three senior men's football teams, five junior football teams, two ladies' football teams, four senior hurling teams and two camogie teams. A total of 13 adult clubs now call the city home – Erin Rovers, Erin's Own, Harry Boland's, John McBride's, Limerick, Michael Cusack's, Padraig Pearse's, Parnells, Patriots, St Brendan's, St Mary's and Wolfe Tones. It's more than just the Chicago city area, however. In the surrounding areas of the Midwest, clubs have popped up in places as far afield as Milwaukee, Kansas City, Indianapolis, Minneapolis, St Louis, St Paul and South Bend – the home of the famous Notre Dame Fighting Irish – in Indiana. There are somewhere around twenty-six clubs here in all and, of those, six had won North American championship titles the weekend before – four from Chicago, one from Indianapolis and one from Milwaukee.

Across on the east coast, Boston had been hosting the NACB play-offs for the first time since 2003. The Labour Day weekend festival of Gaelic games had been a huge success – the biggest renewal of the event on record since the competition's inception of a play-off system back in 1982. Clubs from twenty-four cities around the country (excluding New York, which has its own board) took part in seventeen different championships, as well as three other new competitions: a shield tournament in ladies' intermediate football and camogie, as well as an over-40s men's event. I wished I'd made it that far, but luckily I'd seen plenty of Boston in three summers I'd spent there, so I knew the place pretty well. The GAA is huge in the city and I had come across many of those involved during my time there. Of course, just like almost everywhere else, the GAA clubhouses were basically the local bars and I'd certainly seen plenty of them.

The three main clubs I had come across had been the McAnespie's – who play out of the Blackthorn Bar in South Boston – and the Wolfe Tones men's football and Shamrocks ladies' clubs, who both called the Banshee Bar on Dorchester Avenue home. One thing I had learned on my little adventure was that everywhere in the GAA world is linked with somewhere else in some strange way. I was still astonished, however, to learn that the McAnespie's club and the Cormac McAnallen's club in Sydney had actually gone head-to-head back in Aghaloo, Tyrone, earlier that year. In February 2008, a challenge game had been organised to mark the 20th anniversary of the death of Aidan McAnespie, a 24 year old who had been shot dead by a British soldier on his way to the Aghaloo GAA grounds back in 1988. Famous figures such as Derry stars Joe Brolly and Anthony Tohill, Tyrone's Chris Lawn and Peter Canavan, and even current Down star Bennie Coulter had shown up to tog out for the special game. It had certainly been a day to remember, by all accounts.

But back to the NACB championships taking place in the splendid surrounds of the Irish Cultural Centre in Canton. McAnespie's had become the biggest club in the city since its foundation in 1995 and, to cap off a wonderful 2008, they had just added a North American Senior Football Championship to their collection on home soil. After beating Kevin Barry's of Philadelphia in the semi-final, they had gone on to hammer Sean Tracy's of San Francisco in the decider. It had actually been a good weekend for Boston clubs overall, as they had also secured two other titles: Boston Kerry had beaten Boston Galway in the intermediate final, and Boston Roscommon's ladies' team had taken home the senior football crown.

Honours elsewhere had been shared evenly around the country. A total of ten different cities had claimed titles altogether, with Chicago landing four (senior hurling, senior camogie, men's Junior C football and ladies' Junior B football), San Francisco bringing three home to the west coast, and Philadelphia claiming two trophies (the All American-born football championship and the Junior A hurling title). Meanwhile, Austin (men's Junior D football), Charlotte in North Carolina (men's Junior B football), Indianapolis (Junior C hurling), Milwaukee (Junior B hurling) and Washington DC (ladies' Junior A football) had taken home one each. Quite the spread.

One of the great success stories had been that of Milwaukee up the road. Back in July, Sean Ryan of the *Sunday Independent* had written a story about one of the club's founders, Dave Olson. Olson, an American-born builder of Swedish stock, had developed a passion for hurling about 12 years previously after meeting a few Irish lads in his local bar in Wisconsin. Olson had become hooked on the game after reading all about it and watching tapes of All-Ireland finals. From there, the love of the game had grown and grown, and now, rather incredibly, the Milwaukee Hurling Club have over 250 players on their books – only three of whom were born in Ireland.

The club had won their first-ever men's championship (Junior B) the year before, and now a year later they had retained it. Outside of those two most notable achievements, though, the club had also been successful in promoting the game of camogie – although the word 'successful' is somewhat of an understatement. They have now won two North American Championships. Hurling and camogie are alive and well in Wisconsin. Who would have thought it?

Milwaukee isn't the only unlikely GAA heartland with an interesting story to tell, though. Charlotte GAA in North Carolina only began life back in 2001. After early struggles at NACB championships in Chicago and Boston in 2002 and 2003 respectively (they could only gather 11 players in 2003), they had made their breakthrough in Boulder in 2004. The introduction of a junior D football competition at the national championships had been a godsend for struggling smaller GAA cities such as Charlotte, and the Carolina men had been the first to take advantage. In 2004, they defeated Phoenix to win their first-ever North American title. By 2005, they had risen to the ranks of the Junior C competition, and by 2006 they had won it out at the games in Philadelphia. Now, just eight years later, they had won a junior B championship. Meteoric. The club now has two adult men's teams, and a ladies' football team has also been started. There may be no stopping the spread of Charlotte's web.

In Indiana, the rise and rise of the Indianapolis Hurling Club had been equally astounding. The first hurling match had been played in the city back in 2002 – at a wedding, believe it or not. A club was formed in the aftermath of that sevens game, but it wasn't until late 2005 that the club really began to take root. Dubliner Neal Mulrooney and Longford native Shane Powell became the unlikely men behind the club's resurgence, and the main early events in the club calendar revolved around the clash of two local pubs. In the first game of note back in 2006, Pat Flynn's Pub had beaten Connor's Pub to claim the Spring Indianapolis Celtic Cup on a scoreline of 5–15 to 3–8. You couldn't make it up. Now they had taken the game to a national level and claimed an NACB Junior C Hurling Championship. Outstanding.

I found myself bitterly regretting I had not been there in Boston to take it all in. The sight of 30 players running around a field with hurleys and screaming at one another to 'pull', 'block' and 'hook' in an American accent would have been music to the soul. Spilt milk and all that, though. You can't be everywhere, I convinced myself. It wasn't all over yet, anyway.

I'd almost completed a full lap around the globe, and the end of my journey was finally in sight. Last stop: the Big Apple.

13

THE BIG APPLE

THURSDAY, 4 SEPTEMBER 2008 – NEW YORK

I hadn't left the tremendously entertaining and welcoming company of Trevor, Mick and the lads in Chicago quite as early as I had been supposed to the night before. They knew how little time I had in Chicago and were keen to give me a glimpse of the nightlife while they could. Needless to say, it had been a heavy one. The last thing I remembered was landing back at the hostel at 5 a.m. and setting about packing my stuff for a flight to New York. I just about made it to O'Hare, which lies about an hour away in a cab, and despite some rather overly exuberant security measures had successfully boarded my flight. They seem to be a bit more paranoid when you're heading towards New York, for some reason. And I got the impression they pick on those who, like myself at the time, were as sick as ten episodes of *Chicago Hope*.

I landed in JFK at daybreak but had no intention of spending my few days there cramped up in another crappy hostel. That weekend I'd splash out on the Holiday Inn Express in Long Island City. Hey, big spender!

I reckoned I was finally right again from the jetlag, and it was not a huge transition from Central to Eastern time in the States. It was probably just the heavy night in Chicago that did the damage. A lot of damage. Still, in the comfy surrounds of the hotel, which had cable television and an Internet port, I holed myself up for the next few days and got to work on writing up what I'd learned in the past week and a half in New Zealand, San Francisco and Chicago.

The only distraction that first night would come through my increasingly worrying fixation with the American presidential elections. It's must-watch television, and that night's proceedings were set to provide a real highlight in the campaign. At 8 p.m. Eastern, much to my amusement, I was introduced to Sarah Palin at the Republican Convention, by howdy. Was I glued to the screen for the entire night, soaking up every little morsel of political analysis on CNN or any other network I could get my hands on? You betcha!

SUNDAY, 7 SEPTEMBER 2008

Early Sunday morning, I rose fresh as a daisy. It wasn't just any Sunday morning, though. It was the first Sunday in September. And we all know what that means: All-Ireland hurling final day in Croke Park. It usually takes something monumental to get me out of the leaba at such a godforsaken hour; this was one of those things. Having been to New York four times before, I knew just where to head to watch the match.

McLean Avenue in the Bronx is the largest Irish centre in New York. It's the Big Apple's equivalent of Dorchester Avenue in Boston, on which sits a seemingly unending string of Irish bars as far as the eye can see. On this particular Sunday morning, though, I was heading for a renowned hurling haunt. Clarke's Bar sponsors the Offaly senior hurling team, and just two weeks previously the Faithful men had landed the senior hurling title with a 1–18 to 0–14 win over Tipperary. I got the distinct feeling that the celebrations had only just recently finished up.

I landed just in time for the second half of the All-Ireland minor final and forked over my US$20 to the Setanta Sports man at the door. It's amazing to think that on the other side of the planet in Sydney I could be watching the game from the comfort of my living room for just A$15 per month, whereas five hours by plane across the ocean from Dublin I still had to pay in at the door. Get it together, lads. Anyway, Kilkenny, in typical fashion, robbed poor old Galway blind at the death to secure yet another title. At least it was entertaining, which is more than could be said for what was to follow.

The distinct lack of Waterford jerseys knocking around the place had me suspicious from the off. They were either staying away from what they knew was to come, or they had all gone home to Ireland to watch it. I was just hoping they had their eyes closed and a fill of beer in them before they sat down to watch the game that was to follow. The Deise lads had seemingly used up the last of the gas in the semi-final against Tipperary a few weeks earlier, and Kilkenny happily waltzed in to sweep up the pieces on their way to securing a third Liam McCarthy on the trot. It was hardly a shock. The only surprise in my mind was how anyone other than 15 Kilkenny men could be named on the All Stars team. It had really just been the manner of Waterford's capitulation that had been the most disappointing thing for those of us who had got up at the crack of dawn for the pleasure of watching it. I looked in the direction of the Setanta man, but somehow I doubted I'd be getting my money back.

The crowds soon began to disperse away from Clarke's, as the boys in the RTÉ studio were still rummaging through the bones of yet another Kilkenny romp. The bars had been weirdly quiet that morning. I'd been used to heading down to the pubs in Boston at stupid o'clock to watch the games from Ireland, but I'd never seen a worse atmosphere at a game in the US. Probably best we all put that game behind us.

Of course, talk at the bar would turn to who could stop the marauding Cats from claiming fourth, fifth and maybe even ninth in a row. Probably best not to think about that either.

Only about ten people remain in the bar as the television turns to pursuits more local. At the time, the NFL season was kicking off and one story was big news in New York – particularly in this part of the city. The New York Giants were the reigning Super Bowl champions and had kicked off their season with a win on the Thursday night in Giants Stadium in New Jersey. The game had clashed with the debut of a certain lipsticked bulldog from Alaska – ouch for the ratings – but with the Giants now up and running (if largely unnoticed in the mainstream), all eyes were trained on the New York Jets. And, more pertinently, their new quarter-back. Brett Favre (the guy from *There's Something About Mary*) had come from the storied franchise of the Packers in Green Bay, Wisconsin, and was giving it one more shot at the big-time before hanging up his spurs. I was intrigued by the spectacle. It was quite hard not to be. What I lacked in detail on the event was duly filled by the barman.

Dave Hutton, from Dunboyne in Co. Meath, had been in the US for more than 20 years. He'd grown up 200 yards down the road from my grandmother, it would soon emerge, and he was a cousin of some family friends. Yep, you've guessed what's coming next. Small, small aul world.

I eventually tore myself away from the Jets game long enough to say farewell to Dave and head for the cab he'd called me. I was off to that Mecca of international GAA – probably *the* Mecca of the GAA abroad, to be fair – Gaelic Park in New York City.

It was junior A football championship final day and the crowds were gathering en masse at the famous ground. The place has gone by a few different names over the years – including Innisfáil Park – but since the 1950s it has been Gaelic Park. It had been in danger of falling out of use in the 1930s and the association here toyed with bankruptcy; however, in 1941 the GAA took up the lease again. That legend of the game John 'Kerry' O'Donnell stepped in to save the day, and in the next few years annals of historic clashes were written in its soil.

The legendary Dublin–Kerry rivalry of the late '70s had a chapter written there in a pre-season game in 1978. Kerry, upset about the happenings in the previous year's All-Ireland semi-final, which they'd lost to Dublin, came looking for reparations. A bloodbath ensued that would darken the feud between the sides – a day perhaps many New York GAA people would rather forget.

The details of just what happened that day differ somewhat depending on the teller, but I think it's safe to say there was some pretty nasty stuff. Tom Humphries, in his book *Dublin v Kerry*, actually goes into a little more detail on exactly what happened, but the accounts I'm given in New York range from LA riots to schoolyard fisticuffs. I guess it was just one of those occasions where you had to be there or you'd never really know – the kind of thing that would crash Joe Duffy's phonelines if it happened today. But those were different times; times when men were men, and angry mothers cried out not in anguish or in horror, but for blood and retribution for their injured sons and daughters. Some would say better times. The modern-day majority probably not so much.

A few years previously, however, the stadium had enjoyed its proudest day. In 1947, Cavan took on Kerry in the All-Ireland Senior Football Championship final – the game being staged in New York to commemorate the anniversary of the Great Famine. Cavan emerged victorious on what had been a red-letter day for many whose families had fled the great disaster more than a century before.

There is no shortage of great stories to have emerged from this famous ground, but one tale tickled my fancy in particular. An Australian team of AFL stars had come to Gaelic Park in the winter of 1967 after a successful International Rules tour of Ireland and Britain – the first of its kind, which became known as the Australian World Football Tour – in which they'd beaten all-comers thus far. The final leg on that trip had taken them to the US and they were due to face a New York selection on a dirty day in Gaelic Park. One of the stars of the local GAA in the Big Apple at the time was a local NYPD officer named Brendan Tumulty. Aussie star Ron Barassi that day lined out to mark him. There was friction in the air.

Barassi is an infamous figure in Aussie Rules circles to this day, but his legacy in building friendships between the GAA and the

159

AFL has also been immense. When Tadhg Kennelly first came to Sydney in 1999, he received the Ron Barassi Scholarship, an award created especially for the Kerryman. It had been the first time that an Irish youngster had come out to play Aussie Rules since Jim Stynes and the AFL were determined to do it right. The scholarship effectively covered Tadhg's costs of attending New South Wales University. The idea was that if Kennelly came to Oz and failed in his pursuits as a player, he would at least return to Ireland with some sort of an education. It's one of the things that rarely gets mentioned in Ireland when doomsayers are fretting over the AFL and their Pied Piper scouts. When Brendan Murphy joined Kennelly there in 2007, Barassi was on hand to present him with the prize in person.

The player of the tournament in the now defunct Ireland v. Australia under-17 International Rules Test series was awarded with a prize named in his honour – the Ron Barassi medal. The Victoria native's philanthropic contributions off the field have been immense, but on the field it was no-holds-barred stuff every minute of every game. All or nothing. Life or death. Old-school hardman footie.

On that particular day in New York, Barassi – who in his prime stood less than five foot nine and weighed just over thirteen stone – had come to play in a serious way. He was fearless and everyone who knew him or of him was aware of his colourful 'techniques' of unhinging opponents. Tumulty, however, a policeman of Irish descent who stood well over six foot three, had never heard of him.

This was no exhibition match either. Both sides had come to play. The Aussies had an unbeaten tour to complete, while the New Yorkers wanted to be the only team to beat them. Two fingers up to the star-studded inter-county sides in Ireland that had failed to do the same. This was set to be a game for the ages and the battle between the giant NYPD cop and the diminutive, terrier-like Barassi summed it up.

The first ball that came between the pair flew in about seven feet off the ground, a delivery suited to the American, with the height and weight advantage. Barassi swung from behind with a closed fist but missed the ball, low, by about a foot. Tumulty, unhappy to say the least, arose from the ground and shook off the stars long enough to vent his displeasure. 'Do it again, boyo, and I'll bury you' was the reported gist of it. This is a family book. Barassi stood his ground and smiled in the big man's face. 'Take your free.'

Things were edgy all over the field that day, even in the early stages. The slightest spark was all the place needed to combust.

Then the next ball came in high to Tumulty once again. Bang. The big policeman hit the deck with a thud but didn't stay down long. He rose to his feet and turned his attentions to Barassi. His protestations of displeasure had now reached the point where words would no longer do. It was on.

Reports get a bit sketchy from this point. But Barassi recalls the scene in the aftermath at the local hospital. 'Four of us, two from each side, met at the local hospital for X-rays. Hassa Mann had a broken jaw. One little red-headed Irishman had cracked ribs. I had a cracked nose given to me by Brendan Tumulty, who had a broken thumb from thumping me.' A few years later when the war in Gaelic Park had long been forgotten, Ron Barassi appeared on the Australian version of *This Is Your Life*. The crowd, and his friends and family, had all gathered to celebrate his amazing career over the course of which he had won six Premiership titles as a player with the Melbourne Demons, captaining the team to two of them. He had also won four Premierships as a coach, and it is for these achievements that he had become so well known. Dignitaries from all walks of life and from throughout his career had shown up to pay their respects, but in the midst of it all one producer thought it might be entertaining to mix things up a little. Maybe he'd been told a different version of events at Gaelic Park all those years before. Either way, before Barassi knew what was going on Tumulty had been introduced and stepped out from behind the curtain. The two men smiled at one another in mutual recognition of the real story behind their first meeting. Since that point their respective families have gone on holidays together on a regular basis. An amazing story. Sport really can bring people together – especially under the strangest of circumstances.

Gaelic Park rolled along just fine after that until it was taken over by Manhattan College in 1991 – the scoreboard duly reflects the fact that American Football games are also still regularly played there in the winter. In early 2007, the ground was converted to AstroTurf and along with that development came floodlights. A massive step forward. It's a little sad to think that the GAA don't actually own this pitch, or the bar that sits in the corner of the ground, but it's still a special place to visit, considering all the history that has unfolded here over the years. That day in September 2008, though, two clubs would be out to make history of their own.

It was to be Tyrone's day, as they saw off the challenge of a gallant St Raymond's team. For the Red Hand club, sponsored by Ned Devine's (just across the road from Clarke's on McLean Avenue), it would be their third title on the trot. I got the impression Ned's mightn't be a bad spot for a pint that evening.

It hadn't just been the junior A final that had been contested that day; there had been a full programme of football games, and I'd hung around to watch the last of the day, as Leitrim beat Four Provinces in a senior football championship play-off. The standard was surprisingly high and the atmosphere probably the best I'd seen at games anywhere outside Ireland. It seemed a really traditional way to spend a Sunday afternoon. Long may that continue.

After the final whistle in the Leitrim game, I strode across the park to track down Eugene Kyne. The Claregalway man had been the New York GAA public relations officer and I was keen to pick his brains. I'd finally tracked him down as he was leaving the press box on the far side of the field. A large part of his role in public relations was doing the match reports from the games every weekend for the local papers. He was in a hurry as I caught up with him, but he'd known I was coming and so duly arranged to meet me in the city the following night. I was happy with that plan. It seemed an ideal way to wrap things up on my final day in the Big Apple.

THE BIG APPLE

The size and scale of the GAA in New York is really quite astounding. I had decided well in advance not to even try to take on the overall subject of its storied history and instead merely take a sample of a weekend of GAA life. Eugene Kyne was just the kind of person I'd been hoping to speak to – a committed GAA man more interested in the future of the games here than in their past or their politics. A dual star in his day, Eugene is a member of the Astoria Gaels club and a Tribesman to boot. The only detail I'd known about him before landing had been that he was the public relations guy of New York GAA. I would soon discover that he had, in fact, vacated that position the week before after a row with the County Board. Politics, he tells me. Something to do with match tickets. I'm not touching that one with a barge pole.

It's an interesting sidenote nonetheless and led me to an observation – the bigger the association gets in any given place, the more problems that seem to arise. And the more arguments over things like match tickets. Thankfully, it's for the love of Gaelic games that Kyne had become involved in the first place. And if not for people like him the GAA landscape would be a much darker place, forever choking on its own internal wranglings.

I met up with Eugene that evening in Annie Moore's in Manhattan, just around the corner from Grand Central Station. The bar is quite a famous one and is owned by a Kilkenny man by the name of Tom Ryan. A cosy spot, it's a kind of sanctuary away from the bustling madness of the city that never sleeps on a Monday evening at finishing time. I was certainly comfy tucking into a burger and a pint of Guinness at the bar. I could be anywhere. New York is incomparable to any other city in the US in that regard. It is its own little planet within which different communities from all corners of the globe reside. It's America's heartland, in a way, a sheer testament to the immigration on which the country has been built. At the same time, it lives by its own rules. After 9/11, you would sometimes hear talk of Americans uniting in compassion, love and support for one another – but more often than not it was about 'New Yorkers' and the sense of community they had shown. America wasn't attacked, some would tell you, New York was. In the mind of your average Big Apple native, there's NYC and then there's everywhere else. Whether this New York mindset had anything to do with it or not, the New York County Board had long since become a completely separate entity from the North American equivalent. The two organisations actually had very little interaction, but the one area in which they did was perhaps the most crucial – the Continental Youth Championships.

The CYC had been held just down the road in Philadelphia that July and it was a massive event. Philadelphia, incidentally, is where Four Provinces hail from, the club that had lost to Leitrim the day before. Galway senior Michael Donnellan had also been in their line-up at one stage earlier in the season. It's not far from New York City, and Kyne had made the short journey there for the CYC, taking his own kids along to the event. He'd even refereed a few games on the day. Children from all over North America, Britain and Ireland had come to Philly to take part in the unique spectacle, and one great story that emerged from the weekend's action had really piqued my interest – that of the Cúchulainn's hurling team. Pupils from schools across the Belfast Catholic and Protestant communities had come together to form an under-16 hurling team. They travelled to Philly not long after and amazingly beat a team from New York and a combined Chicago/San Francisco/Boston selection to win the CYC title. Heart-lifting stuff. I'd thought the sight of two young lads in Celtic and Rangers jerseys pucking around in Singapore had been a step in the right direction. I'm clearly way behind the times.

The CYC had been a massive success story. It had been the biggest championships in the event's five-year history, with a total of 236 games played over three days. More than 115 football teams and nine hurling teams, representing twelve cities from the US, Canada, Britain and Ireland, had all taken part. Teams had come from as far and wide as Boston, Chicago, Detroit,

New Haven in Connecticut, New York, Ottawa and Toronto in Canada, Pittsburgh and San Francisco to join the local teams from Philadelphia and take part in competitions from under-8s all the way up to minor. Nickey Brennan and overseas development officer Sheamus Howlin had both been on hand. The two lads couldn't help but be impressed.

The GAA had appointed a paid officer to look after such events earlier that year. Mary Ruane of Chicago club Wolfe Tones had been named as the national games development coordinator for all of North America, a part-time position that also included the role of overseeing the CYC (she had previously been the secretary of the CYC's steering committee). If the tournament in Philly was any indication of what lay in store, it was money well spent. Indeed, Ruane, who was actually born in Middlesex in England and is married to an Athenry man named Adrian, had her own four kids – Brian, Orla, Kieran and Mairead – in action that same weekend. The whole event really was a family affair.

Another interesting aspect of the CYC is that it incorporates not only New York but also teams and players from Canada. The GAA north of the border has a huge history – to the point where it provided the subject for a book by Vancouver author John O'Flynn entitled *The History of the Gaelic Athletic Association in Canada*. It's a tricky book to track down, but in it he traces the history of the association in Canada as far back as 1788 in St John's, Newfoundland. He also makes some very interesting observations, one of them linking hurling to the foundation of the country's national sport, ice hockey. It's a great read, and the story of O'Flynn himself is an interesting one.

He was born in Vancouver in 1964 just two years after his parents – Thomas from Limerick, and Elizabeth from Kerry – had landed there. His love for Gaelic games had grown through their influence and he had attended the founding meeting in Toronto in 1987 of the Canadian County Board. And he went on to write a book about it. It really is a generational thing. Since that meeting, the board in Canada have gone from strength to strength, to the point where there are now roughly 525 registered players within Canada from four Provinces – British Columbia, Alberta, Ontario and Quebec. And with youngsters playing in events like the CYC every year, things can only continue to grow.

Back to New York, though, and it's not hard to see the strength in depth of the club game there. In 2008, ten senior football and ten junior football sides (including Kyne's own Astoria Gaels) took part in the big-ball competition. That's as big a selection to choose from as many a county side in Ireland. I found myself wondering why New York hadn't troubled teams more in the Connacht Senior Football Championship – especially considering the standard I'd seen at first hand the day before in Gaelic Park. Controversy a few years earlier – created when New York had reached an Ulster Senior Hurling Championship final rather unexpectedly – might offer the best clue in answering that question, though. The New Yorkers hadn't been expected to win a game in the competition and nobody had thought to really plan for such a scenario. Everyone was delighted for the New York boys, but the complications that arose from it were far-reaching. Usually, New York would enter the Ulster championship and either Derry, Down, Antrim or whoever else they got in the draw would hop on the plane to Gaelic Park. The local boys would put up a good fight, and everyone would get their day out, but the winner – always the visitors in modern times – would return home to play the next round of the competition. New York actually winning this game completely threw the cat amongst the pigeons. The Big Apple boys now had to travel back to Ireland to play the next round, but not all of them could make it. There were several reasons given, but one of the most likely is that some of the boys might have been illegal immigrants living in the city – many of whom would have missed many birthdays, funerals and weddings over the years – knowing they could never get back into the US again had they returned to Ireland. Winning a match was great and all, but the odds of getting those same 15 New York players on the field again in Casement Park in Belfast were astronomical. For whatever reason.

It was suggested that Antrim should play in New York instead. Antrim refused. And so it went back and forth. Both sides had real and valid arguments, but a resolution was no closer.

The controversy would have been huge had this happened in the football championship as opposed to its oft-neglected although better-looking cousin. The same question can just as easily be asked, though. If the New York footballers were to actually ambush someone in the first round of the Connacht Football Championship, which they play at Gaelic Park every year, could they realistically bring an equally strong team back to Ireland to play in the next round? Considering what I'd learned from Billy Lawless in Chicago, and the fact that the sister organisation of the Irish illegal group here dwarfs the one in Illinois, the answer is probably not. If there were illegal lads on the team – and I'm not saying there were – they just wouldn't take the risk of returning home for the sake of a football match. Or a hurling match, for that matter. Not in the age of the Patriot Act.

That's not to say this will always be the case. The people of America, and even the Irish illegals who hadn't voted for Obama, had been promised change they could believe in. I'm fully convinced that in an ideal world, with no visa issues, and if New York could put out the strongest team available to them at any given time, they'd trouble many a county senior side. Sadly, we may never know.

It had been a great weekend in New York and I'd learned a lot, but the urge for the taste of Irish soil had gripped by this stage. I was just one flight away from completing a full lap of the world. Nine countries and eighteen cities later, I was finally on my way home to where it had all begun. It would be great to see old friends and family again – but after just three days back in the motherland, I was straight back to work in Sydney. Still, could be worse, eh?

AUSTRALASIA
REVISITED

14

INTERNATIONAL RULES

It was 8 a.m. as my flight landed at Sydney airport. It had been a hectic few weeks but it was straight back to the grindstone, though it was hard to complain about heading into summer Down Under as the bleakness of winter began to loom over the summer evenings in Dublin. I'd had a busy few days meeting friends and family, but after catching my home club's senior football team in action in the Dublin championship it was straight to the airport and off back to Australia. I'd left at 9 p.m. on Saturday and was just landing in New South Wales then. I was due in work an hour later. If only they sold sleep in packets.

The flight had been a blessing, though. Just 12 months earlier I had never heard of Etihad Airways. Now, they had all but revolutionised the journey linking Ireland and Australia, as well as having become the new major sponsors of the All-Ireland Senior Hurling Championship. Their one-stop flights to Sydney, Melbourne and Brisbane had cut out the middleman in London. Unless you've flown on the Dublin/London/Bangkok/Sydney 24-hour merry-go-round it's hard to appreciate the blessing of such a bypass. They're not paying me to say this either, by the way.

Not much had happened since I'd left, other than that Tadhg Kennelly's Swans had got knocked out of the AFL play-offs. Kennelly had soldiered on through knee and shoulder injuries into the post-season, but Sydney's run had come to an end at the

171

hands of the Western Bulldogs the previous Friday. Had the Swans gone further into the play-offs, Kennelly could have postponed the surgery he needed on both his groin and shoulder. As it was, he had to make a call. His dream of captaining Ireland in the International Rules series was over. In the end, he went for the surgery.

His counterparts in Kerry, meanwhile, had one more game to go in their season.

SUNDAY, 21 SEPTEMBER 2008

All-Ireland football final day and the Cormac McAnallen's GAA club had organised a barbecue on Bondi Beach. It was a beautiful day and the club's members were excited about the game ahead. Founded by Tyrone men and named after one, it's hardly surprising to learn that most of the players and members are also from the Red Hand county. The atmosphere was reaching fever pitch as the sun made its dying bows on the horizon.

I spotted Tadhg Kennelly across the way and headed over for a chat. He had just had the operation on his groin but was walking around unhindered. He said it had all gone well, but he still had the shoulder surgery ahead.

It had been a nightmare season for the Kerryman – he had dislocated his kneecap in one game before going on to dislocate his shoulder a few games later. He had made onfield efforts to pop both back in at the time. It hadn't been a pretty sight. At least now it was all going to be put into the hands of professionals. He was determined to be right for the following season with the Swans, his last contracted year with the club, but, as ever, remained elusive about his future in the AFL. He wouldn't confirm that 2009 would be his last season at the club, but he wouldn't deny it either. He maintained he still harboured ambitions of winning All-Irelands with Kerry. His time was running out, though, and he knew it.

His housemate, Swans' Carlow rookie Brendan Murphy, had already gone home to Ireland, while his newest clubmate in Sydney, Tyrone minor star Kyle Coney, was readying himself for an All-

Ireland minor final that night. Sydney coach Paul Roos had offered Tadhg the chance to go home and watch the All-Ireland final live and in person, had he wanted to. Kennelly had knocked him back. The only thing more painful than watching Kerry in an All-Ireland final on television from Australia, he reckoned, was watching them from the stands at Croker and not being able to run on and kick a ball. The rest of us were just glad to have television coverage.

Although Setanta Sports show almost all the GAA games live and available to homes in Australia, most people like to go out for All-Ireland final night, obviously enough, for the atmosphere. Unfortunately, Sydney isn't exactly thronging with places to watch GAA games. In Melbourne, they have the Celtic Club; in Perth, the Irish Club; in Canberra and Brisbane, the same. In Sydney, however, no such place exists. It used to, once upon a time, but that's another story altogether. These days only two Irish bars in the entire city stay open past midnight on a Sunday – Scruffy Murphy's and Paddy Maguire's. Both are favoured haunts of backpackers and so the atmosphere tends to be somewhat 'festive' come throw-in time at 1 a.m. Usually they're places I'm happy to avoid. I was worried I would have to make an exception for that night's game, but thankfully I learned that a third option had reared its head. A new bar was having its first late-night opening.

Madame De Biers in Kings Cross might not sound like much of an Irish bar – and, in truth, it isn't – but it is owned by the PJ O'Brien's pub group. The group's owner, Paul O'Brien, is a proud Irish-Australian and he and PJ's licensee, Fergal McCauley, had been heavily involved in supporting the NSW GAA, while they also sponsored the McAnallen's GAA club. Unfortunately, PJ's main bar in the city closed early on Sunday nights due to licensing restrictions and so it couldn't live out its potential as the GAA bar it was surely born to be. It was through the PJ's connection with McAnallen's that the rest of us had learned of the planned late-night opening in Kings Cross. For one night only, Madame De Biers would be thronged with GAA jerseys.

The minor final was a thriller and we had landed there in plenty of time to take it in. There were pockets of Mayo jerseys scattered around, but for the most part people on the street hadn't heard about this place and so the balance was tilted heavily in Tyrone's favour. I'd met a friend of mine, Down man Micky Quail, who runs the whosyourpaddy.com backpacker website in Australia, and we'd secured a seat upstairs in front of the big screen. It was nice and calm, and we could only imagine how busy Scruffy's and Maguire's must have been. We were immersed in the minor game, though, which finished in a draw. Sydney Swans recruit Coney would score five points from play in a man-of-the-match display in Tyrone's replay win. Not a bad way to end your GAA career. For the time being, at least.

The senior game threw up another thriller. The Tyrone fans – hundreds of them – had been screaming and bawling all through the game downstairs, as Kennelly and a few of his fellow Kingdom natives had sat contemplatively away from the eyes of the Red Hand majority. Probably for the best, in the end. The last thing I remember seeing was a Tadhg Kennelly-shaped hole in Madame De Biers' front door. It was all getting a bit rowdy downstairs, so I quickly decided to follow suit. If there's no Kerrymen around to take the slagging, the Dubs are normally next in line. After 13 years of misery, I was becoming a little too fragile to take it any more.

There was nowhere to hide from Tyrone people in Sydney, though. It'd be at least another 12 months until any of us had heard the end of this one.

SUNDAY, 5 OCTOBER 2008

Everything had by now been wrapped up at home in GAA land, with Tyrone and Kilkenny having sewn up the big ones in the weeks gone by. In Australia, though, there were two major events left on the sporting calendar. Sunday, 5 October was the culmination of the first.

The annual State Games had been going on in Adelaide since

that Monday and now the finals were to be decided. The State Games are quite a simple concept, really. They are the equivalent of inter-county at home, basically – the best players are chosen to represent their state from the respective clubs in each of the major cities. The standard is usually fairly high, depending on who's around at the time. For example, earlier in the year I'd run into Dublin senior dual star David 'Dotsy' O'Callaghan in the Cock 'n Bull in Sydney. In the previous six months or so, he'd come from playing football in Boston with the Wolfe Tones club to lining out with Victoria in the State Games. As I met him, he was on his way back home to hurl for the Dubs. In the middle of the 2007 season, he'd called time on his efforts to make the Dublin footballers' almost impenetrable first 15. In July 2008, he went on to win the Hurler of the Month award. Not a bad few months, in anyone's book. Certainly fits well with this one.

In 2008, players of Dotsy's inter-county standard weren't as likely to make the journey for the Games. The city of Adelaide, which sits in South Australia, is a tricky spot to get to, and in some cases an expensive one, too. Auckland, for example, wouldn't even send a team. Playing football in the Games also involves taking a week off work and many people just aren't willing to do that. All the same, six teams had travelled to play in the senior football event – Western Australia, Victoria, Queensland and New South Wales would join New Zealand side Wellington/Hutt Valley and hosts South Australia. They, and 400 other Gaels, had called the Westminster School in the South Australian capital their home for the week.

Australasian County Board secretary Gerard Roe had given the *Irish Echo* a list of championship previews the previous week. He reckoned NSW would be favourites to win the men's football title for the fifth time in six years. The Blues had been spearheaded by Castleisland native Kevin Lynch the year before – he had scored a whopping 2–8 in the final win over Victoria – and the Clan na Gael club man was just back after getting married a few weeks earlier (turned out he was a mate of Trevor and Mick O'Donoghue's from the Kerryman Bar in Chicago, and had met up with the boys along the way). With the biggest population and the largest number of football clubs on the continent, it seemed to make sense that NSW would be favourites. It wouldn't work out that way, though. Ah, the beauty of the GAA.

NSW were stymied as a result of a rule passed by the Australasian Board. In an effort to level the playing field, it had been decided that a minimum number of permanent residents of Australia must constitute the playing squad of each state team. The problem for NSW – and indeed for Victoria, who had also voted against such a move – was that backpackers made up the core of their leagues in Sydney and Melbourne respectively. In Australia, there also exists a kind of middle tier between a backpacker who's there for a year and another who has permanent residency. Some backpackers come with a working-holiday visa but are sponsored by a company to stay on and live and work there for four years. Under the new rules, those on sponsorship visas were to be counted in the same breath as 'backpackers'.

NSW and Victoria were not amused. They'd lost most of their panels. Indeed, the New South Welshmen had struggled to even get a team together under the rule. Their goalkeeper, a young sports writer called Edwin McGreal from Mayo, had reported that fewer than 15 players had been training with the team at one point just a few weeks before the games. In the end, because he was also a backpacker, he couldn't even play himself. The intention of the board had been to level the playing fields for the other states. And, in fairness, it had done just that. But they'd also cut out a lot of others who had every right to be involved. Most of the members of the committee in NSW were in the country on sponsorship visas.

Victoria, it would emerge, had somehow adapted best. After a tough week of competition, they had reached the final to face the tournament's biggest surprise package – hosts South Australia. Incredibly, for a competition that had once attracted inter-county footballers such as O'Callaghan, the Adelaide boys had beaten Wellington/Hutt Valley by 17 points, NSW by 15 and Queensland by 17 on their way to the final. The incredible part of that scenario was that Dubliner Andy Keogh was the only Irishman on the team. Adelaide had been working hard on building their underage structures for years and it was really beginning to pay off. Gerry Roe, before moving to Alice Springs, had been a large part of that back when he still called the South Australian capital home. A team of Australians had beaten – nay, hammered – teams packed with Irish boys. Even more amazingly in the case of their achievement, though, was the fact that their regular club season hadn't even started yet. The leagues and championships in South Australia run in the summer months and don't even get under way until January each year. The Adelaide boys would go on to lose to Victoria by 14 points in the final, but all the same they'd made their mark. And it certainly wasn't an overnight success.

The Gaelic Football and Hurling Association of South Australia was formed in 1967, but it was during the mid-1980s that a steady stream of non-Irish Australian participants of all ethnic backgrounds had begun to join the association. The introduction of a first Adelaide team into the AFL in 1991 had been a massive blow to the GAA in the state, and when a second team was created in 1997 the association was on the brink of collapse. The GAA could no longer play games on Sundays during the winter, as they clashed with AFL games, and so the switch was made to summer leagues instead. Looking at how their almost completely Australian-born team had performed in the State Games, you'd have to say it was working.

In the hurling, whatever about the football, NSW were the all-singing all-dancing kings of the mountain. In fact, you had to look back to 1991 before you found a year when anyone other than the Sydney men had won the event. Only three teams had entered the 2008 competition, with Victoria and Western Australia given the task of putting it up to the champion Blues. Usually Sydney would enter two teams in the State Games – a NSW City team and a NSW Country team – but the new backpacker rule had put paid to those plans. Just like the footballers, they'd struggled to get even one team together. All things said, though, it might have been the best thing for the state of the game in Australia. NSW failed even to make the final and for the first time ever it was Victoria (who have three clubs in Garryowen, Sinn Féin and Shamrocks) and Western Australia (who don't even have a hurling league) fighting it out for national honours. Despite a gallant effort from the Perth men, it was the Vics who secured a men's double, thanks to a narrow two-point win. The signs were certainly pointing in the right direction for the small-ball game, all the same. Especially if the boys can keep it going in Perth.

As is often the case, it was the women's football and camogie that provided the best entertainment. There had been a camogie exhibition game played in the State Games in Sydney the year before, but unfortunately there was no repeat match in Adelaide this time around. The ladies' footballers, however, did light things up on the excitement front. Three teams – NSW, Victoria and SA – were out to stop the all-conquering and reigning three-in-row champions WA. The Perth girls were after an historic fourth State Games title in a row – a feat never before achieved – and it was a hectic week with just one day off between Monday's opening round and Saturday and Sunday's play-offs. Last woman standing. Two teams in particular started as they meant to finish. Hosts SA and WA, after opening with wins over Queensland and NSW respectively, went on to compete in the decider. It turned out to be the game of the week. In a major shock, the girls of South Australia beat the defending champions, thanks to two late points. They had come back from 2–1 to 0–2 down after ten minutes and a point behind with less than five to go. It was epic.

Finally, it was the turn of the minors to crown a champion. Virtually every player in the under-18 competition was born in Australia and three teams were vying to take the title home. After being forced to miss out on the 2007 Games in Sydney, 2006 champions WA were back to reclaim their crown. SA made up the third and final team in the competition, but it was the Vics and the Perth lads who played out an entertaining final. WA came out on top with ten points to spare. All is well for the future there, it seemed. In Victoria, SA and WA anyway.

With the State Games done and dusted, there was only one event left to occupy the minds of the Gaels Down Under – the long-awaited and much anticipated return of the International Rules series. Ding-ding. Round one. Perth.

FRIDAY, 24 OCTOBER 2008 – PERTH

In Australia, at least what we call Irish Australia, the return of the International Rules series had been big news when it had broken in May. I was certainly excited. You don't get to see the cream of Irish Gaelic football up close and personal all that often Down Under and news that Seán Boylan would be taking the reins once again meant we were likely to see our best and brightest on the tour. The Australians had appointed one of their most successful and respected coaches, Mick Malthouse – Marty Clarke's club coach at the country's biggest team, the Collingwood Magpies. I had hoped that his appointment would lead to a top-class sort signing up to pull on the Aussie guernsey (the Aussie Rules sleeveless top). Sadly, we'd all be disappointed in that regard. Malthouse ended up naming a very inexperienced side, with only six of his twenty-five-man squad having played the compromise game previously. He insisted that he and his selectors had gone for 'youth, speed, skill and agility'; however his final squad included just nine of the top fifty players in the AFL, according to the Brownlow Medal rankings. Only one of Malthouse's selection made the top ten in that vote – North Melbourne's Brent Harvey – while only one other player, Adelaide's Scott Thompson, had broken into the top twenty. Only four players from AFL Grand Finalists Hawthorn and Geelong were named in the squad. This was quite simply not the best team Australia had to offer. No matter how Malthouse chose to spin it.

Ireland, on the other hand, had had their strongest players to choose from, with a few exceptions. Marty Clarke missed out through an ankle injury, while Kennelly had been ruled out the month before, leaving Laois's Colm Begley as the sole Irish AFL player in the squad. Aside from these absences, the team was rock solid with heavyweights Sean Cavanagh, Michael Meehan and Graham Canty having made the trip. The travelling team always seemed to bring their best. It was especially true in the case of Australia. The best and brightest in the AFL just wouldn't bother cutting their holidays short if it didn't mean a free trip to Ireland.

Malthouse, to give him his due, is a genuine guy – and a genuine winner. I'd been handed the task of interviewing him ahead of the opening Test match in Perth and I could tell that he genuinely wanted to win that series. His CV is impeccable. He had managed the West Coast Eagles in Perth for nine years, over which time he had never failed to make the play-offs and had won two Premiership titles along the way. He'd been with Collingwood for the previous eight years, in which time he'd won more games than he'd lost. This time around, though, he knew it was about more than winning.

The 2006 debacle in Croke Park, in which the Irish and Australian teams had beaten the heads off one another, had, in many people's eyes, been a case of wounded professional pride lashing out at a perceived lack of respect. The Aussies had been riled after the first Test, which they'd lost in Galway, and in particular by the way they'd been spoken of in the Irish media in the aftermath. At Croker in the second Test, they'd been out to make an example of someone. The entire series had been cancelled as a direct result of the violent scenes which occurred that day back in 2006. This was the first time the series had been played since and a lot was on the line. Malthouse knew the entire future of the International Rules series was in his and Seán Boylan's hands. He had made that point perfectly clear to me. He fully understood the responsibility he had been given and was determined to secure the future of the compromise series for the generations of Aussie Rules footballers yet to come. He genuinely believed in it and he wasn't willing to jeopardise the future of an entire sport – and the only opportunity future AFL players would have to represent their country – under any circumstances. Not even if that ultimately meant losing.

The unpleasantness of 2006 had cast a most unwelcome shadow over the series. At the time, Australians had been mostly put out by the level of outrage in Ireland. The public in Australia basically saw the Irish as having completely over-reacted and blown the whole thing out of all proportion. The GAA, and its fans – in the eyes of the average Aussie at the time – were complete whingers. One man who hadn't been shy in offering his own opinion in that regard was the quintessential Irish-Australian footballing convert himself, Jim Stynes. And he hadn't endeared himself to the Irish community in the process either. The whole thing really got ugly in some quarters. Uglier even than what had happened on the field.

I'd finally managed to catch up with Jim in the days before the first Test in Perth. His new role as Demons chairman was a dream come true, but it was a mountainous task he had taken on. The club was in dire financial straits and the majority of his daily life had been consumed by the task of righting the rocking Melbourne Football Club ship. A lot had changed since his comments in the wake of the 2006 series, of course. One thing that hadn't, however, was his opinion on what had gone wrong that fateful day in Croker. He wasn't angry about it any more, but he hadn't changed his mind about what he believed had caused the whole thing. He still reckoned Ireland's philosophy going into that series had been poor. That Graham Geraghty should have been suspended after the first game in Galway. And that the Irish media's portrayal of the Aussie team as a soft touch had led to a physical backlash from the tourists. Water under the bridge really, though. Or so we all dearly hoped in the lead-up. Jim told me he was looking forward to the series all the same. He'd be at the MCG for the second Test a week later with his wife, kids and all the Stynes family – including brother Brian. I found myself wondering what colour scarves they'd all be wearing.

The last man in my crosshair as the Perth game ticked closer was Boylan. The Meath man has been a hero of mine all my life and I had been delighted to see him retake the challenge of the International Rules coaching job. He had received a lot of criticism for the way his team had behaved – and perhaps, more importantly, how they had played – in the 2006 series. He was determined to make amends – both off the field and on. Things hadn't been good between the two camps in the week between the first and second Tests in Ireland two years previously. Poor organisation and a lack of social interaction meant that the players had only become acquainted through their efforts to thump the heads off one another. That kind of thing doesn't make for a good atmosphere in any situation.

Things looked a lot better this time around and Boylan had been quick to acknowledge that. He was happy with the introduction of functions midweek, at which the players got to know one another a little better outside of the arena. By their respective tones, I certainly got the impression that the Meath man and Malthouse were going to get along just fine. Back in 2006 things hadn't been quite so rosy between Boylan and then Aussie coach Kevin Sheedy.

Sheedy's autobiography, I'm sure by no coincidence, was due to hit the shelves in a few days. He'd taken the opportunity in hand to label Boylan as a 'leprechaun' in the Melbourne media just days before the Perth game. Boylan had laughed it off and refused to be drawn. That was all the free publicity Sheedy would be getting off his back, anyway. He was there to do a job.

The Irish population in Western Australia had been on the rise over the previous few years, as the Celtic Tiger had drawn its final breaths. For Irish workers, and tradesmen in particular, Perth offers a land of plenty. Abounding work opportunities at a time when jobs are beginning to slip away at home. It is hard to gauge just how many Irish people are now living there. The attendance, and colour scheme, at the Subiaco Oval would offer some insight in that regard. More than 35,000 crammed into the Perth ground – home to AFL sides the Eagles and Fremantle Dockers – for what turned out to be a thriller. Perth hadn't exactly been the most fertile stomping ground for Irish sides over the years, yet they would go on to claim their first win in the Western Australia ground in 22 years, and their first on Australian soil since 2003. Ireland were leading by seventeen points four minutes into the final quarter, but the Aussies came back to leave Ireland with the narrowest of one-point leads heading into the decider in Melbourne the following week. The AFL folk in the Aussie Rules capital were finally beginning to take notice. All roads to the MCG seven days later.

FRIDAY, 31 OCTOBER 2008 – MELBOURNE

It had been a busy week in the lead-up to the second Test. Outside of the International Rules series itself there had been much to talk about between the AFL and the GAA. Association chief Nickey Brennan had met with AFL head honcho Andrew Demetriou to discuss, amongst other things, the future of the series going forward and the now red-hot issue of Gaelic footballers being lured Down Under. I had caught up with Brennan during the week and, although somewhat guarded, he had said the meetings had been 'highly productive' and that the GAA had got a 'fair hearing' from the AFL. You got the sense that much more work lay ahead in that regard.

I'd spoken to Brennan a few months earlier, in July, as the player recruitment issue had reached a head in Ireland. People were kicking up a stink, as they felt the youth of Ireland was being pillaged from afar. One particular incident had caused uproar – an AFL agent had decided to make use of a GAA field for an impromptu trial session without permission. Brennan knew he needed to nip things in the bud. It was then that the GAA chief had told me of the plan to have a serious sit-down with the AFL. At the time, the name on everyone's lips was Ricky Nixon.

Nixon was a well-known AFL player in his day and had since turned his hand to player management. He had come up with a scheme to compile a list of the best prospects in Ireland through a series of trials and camps before ranking them and putting them forward as potential recruits to a number of AFL clubs. Nixon, before launching into the whole scheme, had taken the measure of first approaching the GAA for a meeting. Brennan told me that he had appreciated this gesture, but that he remained 'very concerned' about the whole thing. By the end of the year, Nixon and the GAA would no longer be on speaking terms.

The gaze of Irish Australia was directed firmly at the MCG. Many had tuned in the week before in the hope that some sort of melee, like in 2006, might entertain them on their Friday night. Instead, they had been treated to a tight and hard-fought contest that had whetted many previously sceptical appetites. The decision to play these games on a Friday night was still baffling me, though. Surely the GAA could have pushed for a Saturday night throw-in so that people in Ireland could tune in on their Saturday morning? I still haven't got an explanation for that one. Television issues had been a problem before. During the 2005 series in Australia, the games hadn't even been televised in Queensland or NSW. In Sydney, where the largest Irish population reside, they couldn't even watch the game. In 2008, it was the people back in Ireland – barring those who had the luxury of a Friday morning off work – who were being denied the chance. You either want these games to grow and create interest, or you don't. Simple stuff.

The plane to Melbourne on Friday morning had been well populated with county jerseys. It was still early days and so impossible to tell just how many would show up at the MCG that night, but the early indications seemed positive. Had the game been on a Saturday, it would have been simpler to hazard a guess based on the number of people in the Irish bars, but this was an after-work job for the Irish in Melbourne and it would only be from Sydney that any serious number of visitors would be travelling. The plan was to stay with my former Sydney Shamrocks teammates Seamie Farrell and Eddie Butler out in the Irish suburb of St Kilda, and after dropping the stuff out there we headed back for the city – and that famous Melbourne haunt, PJ O'Brien's. It was still hours before kick-off, but the place was thronged. The bar, which is a sister pub to the one in Sydney, sits in a shopping centre on the south bank of the Yarra river. For one night at least it was a beacon to the travelling hordes of Irish fans. It was all starting to get a bit hectic as I took my leave of PJ's and headed towards the stadium. The MCG is about a 15-minute tram ride from Flinders Street station in the heart of the city and it sits alongside the Olympic facilities from the Games back in 1956 – the Olympic Stand stood as part of the MCG for nearly 50 years but was demolished in 2004. The old landmark stadium is visible from the heart of the city.

It was quiet around the MCG as I landed and headed for the press box. The pubs, and not just PJ's, would remain packed to the gills until well into the first quarter. Up in the press box, figures such as Mícheál Ó Muircheartaigh and Jim O'Sullivan of the *Irish Examiner* were standing around discussing the game ahead, while a former colleague of mine at the *Sunday Tribune*, who was now writing for the *Melbourne Age* online, Pat Horan, and one of the foremost AFL writers in Australia, Cavan girl Catherine Murphy, were sharing a coffee. There must have been a separate press box for the Australian hacks. Either that or they just hadn't bothered to show up.

The game itself had received very little promotional coverage in that morning's papers. Everyone was hoping it wasn't an omen. For an event to succeed in Australia, it needed Melbourne. Always has, always will.

The players took the field and a roar went up from the stands. The journalists in the press box were creaking their necks around corners, trying to see where the noise was coming from. I, for one, could only see empty seats. Approaching half-time, Ireland led by 18 points and it looked as though it would be a washout.

The stands had drawn even quieter, but then Australia launched a comeback to thankfully make a game of it. Ireland wouldn't relinquish their lead but going into the final minute Australia pulled back to within a score. In the end, though, Ireland held on for a victory that seemed to mean a lot to them – judging by the players' reactions at the final whistle, at least. The crowd had finally begun to come to life as the minutes ticked away, and it was just in the nick of time. Those of us in the press were now convinced of the 42,823 attendance that had been announced 20 minutes previously. There had only been around 41,000 at the Ireland v. Wallabies rugby union Test in June at the Telstra Dome (Etihad Stadium as of March 2009). It was hard to argue with that for a result. The only thing everyone seemed to agree on was that the MCG was far too big a stage for such a game. The Telstra Dome up the road would certainly have made for a better atmosphere.

All the same, the spirit in which the games were played was exceptional. Much to the delight of the GAA and AFL alike, there had been no need for the newly introduced match review panel to put anyone on report after the first Test. In the grand scheme of the series, it was huge. And then the final act of sportsmanship came. Irish captain Seán Cavanagh accepted the Cormac McAnallen Trophy with a huge smile on his face, but after his teammates had joined him on the makeshift stage in the middle of the ground and given the waiting photographers their fill, the Tyrone man laid the trophy delicately down on the hallowed turf of the MCG. Before any lap of honour was undertaken, the Irish team were going to make sure they shook the hand of every single Australian player – a show of unity between the two squads. The future of the hybrid game, at least for now, secured.

The scenes were genuinely jovial as I reached the Irish dressing-room for the post-match press conference. Mick Malthouse, and his captain Brent Harvey, were inside the conference room speaking to the assembled Aussie media as Cavanagh, Boylan and a few other players chatted with journalists in the mix room outside. There were smiles everywhere, but none wider than that on the face of Nickey Brennan. Boylan, in his usual friendly way, was jumping from Irish journalist to Irish journalist as they stood waiting with their Dictaphones outstretched, relishing the opportunity to ask their own questions away from the frenzy of the press conference to follow. Tadhg Kennelly and Colm Begley were walking around, chatting freely to anyone who'd listen, but after about ten minutes Malthouse and Harvey had vacated the press room and it was time for the coach and captain's final media duty of the tour. With the Cormac McAnallen Trophy glistening on the table in front of the victorious Irish team leaders, it wasn't long before Boylan offered an insight into why this meant so much to him and his team. And to the Tyrone lads on the panel, in particular. The last time Ireland had won an International Rules series, Cormac McAnallen had been playing. Now the trophy, which had been named in his honour, was sitting proudly in front of his friend and former teammate. You could see what it meant in Cavanagh's eyes. And in Boylan's.

Cavanagh spoke emotionally but eloquently about how it felt to be holding the trophy that had been named after his late colleague and how it meant so much to him and the boys from the Red Hand county – the McMahons and Enda McGinley. He was keen to point out, however, that it wasn't just for Tyrone; Cavanagh's vice-captain, Graham Canty, and many others on the Irish squad knew McAnallen well too, he explained. It really wasn't hard to see where the motivation had come from, even if the Irish camp hadn't hinted at it one bit in the build-up.

'Who said this didn't mean anything?' Boylan had opened. 'This is as good as any achievement I've had in my career.' Praise from Caesar. And I'm a Dub.

Just as the press conference was winding down and the three lads on stage – Cavanagh and Boylan having been joined late by Brennan – were answering the final query, an official popped his head in the door with an announcement from the independent match review panel. 'No incidents to report,' he bellowed out to the assembled press corps. And I'd genuinely thought Brennan's smile couldn't get any wider.

SUNDAY, 2 NOVEMBER 2008 – SYDNEY

The party had gone on late into the night at PJ O'Brien's in Southbank. The Irish players had arrived down a few hours after the game and, to be honest, it was a wonder there was any room left for them inside. Tipperary native Avril Mulcahy had been handed the task of trying to organise the night on behalf of the pub and she was standing at the front door handing out wristbands as I arrived. She threw me a smile and was beckoning me through the massing hordes towards the door when I spotted a small figure out of the corner of my eye down the corridor. Seán Boylan was standing chatting away to a couple of older lads in Ireland scarves, merrily explaining how much he'd enjoyed his trip to Oz. A group of queuing fans had recognised him and approached, requesting photographs. Boylan duly obliged. His young son hadn't left his side all week, and although it was getting late in the night the Meath man seemed determined to soak it all up. The atmosphere was electric. Boylan would eventually have to tear himself away, however. He, and the Irish team, had a flight to Sydney in the morning.

NSW GAA chairman Brian Deane had told me a few weeks previously that the Irish team would be coming to Sydney to take on a local NSW selection out in Auburn. After the initial agreement between Nickey Brennan and Andrew Demetriou to rekindle the compromise game, the GAA had put in a request that one of the Tests be held in Sydney. The AFL, which was planning to start up a second team in the city, seemed happy to try its best to oblige. But it wouldn't have much luck.

Although Sydney houses the largest Irish population in Australia, it's also the spiritual home of rugby league. The Rugby League World Cup had just kicked off the week before and the organisation responsible for bringing major occasions to Sydney, Events NSW, had knocked back the advances of the AFL. They simply didn't want a circus in town taking away from their big showpiece. The official answer to the AFL's request had been to say that ANZ Stadium (the former Olympic venue) could be made available to host a game, but only under the proviso that it be a stand-alone Sydney fixture. Basically, they'd host it only on the understanding that there be no second Test in Melbourne. The AFL, of course, declined. ANZ Stadium director

Kyle Patterson had been understandably dismayed. The stadium had been seriously struggling and had even reached the point where it was now paying NRL teams, and even the Swans, to come out and play some of their games there. A *Sydney Morning Herald* story had quoted an AFL source as saying that Events NSW had refused funding support for the proposed event, but Sally Edwards, the general manager of operations and communications at Events NSW, told me that they would have supported a Test match had it been a stand-alone fixture in Sydney. A one-off fixture in Sydney, she explained, would have brought a large influx of visitors from Victoria. This prospect, however, became far less appealing when a second Test was pencilled in for Melbourne. Of course the AFL was going to play a game in its heartland. And Events NSW knew that. Politics.

A crowd of around 50,000 could have been reasonably expected to attend a Test match in Sydney, especially considering the large number of international visitors from Ireland who had been seen on the last tour Down Under in 2005. Ireland were also due to open their Rugby League World Cup campaign in the city on 27 October. As far as I could see, the planets had aligned for all parties. Politics, however, had once again stuck its ugly snout into the sporting world – and once again it was the fans who suffered as a result.

Nonetheless, the GAA had remained determined to bring their travelling show to the city. And, much to the credit of Brennan and co., they would do just that. It had been hoped that maybe ten, if we were lucky, of the Irish touring squad might tear themselves away from the party in Melbourne long enough to board a flight to NSW. Much to everyone's delight, and to the credit of Boylan and his players, twenty-two of them would make the journey north. I suspect the promise of a night on the tiles from one Tadhg Kennelly might have held some sway in that decision. I suppose that also counts as politics.

A decent crowd was gathered out in Auburn on a glorious Sunday morning as Boylan's team emerged from the dressing-rooms to a big roar. The Irish boys had downed a few the night before, you got the feeling. And sure, why not? The NSW selection chosen to play them, however, were treating this as life or death. It was a team loaded with Tyrone men. The Blues captain on the day was Cathal McKenna from the McAnallen's club and the team also included several All Stars selections from the State Games Championships earlier that month – one from Wellington, three from Queensland, three from South Australia and one each from Western Australia and Victoria. Five native Australians were also included in the side. The warm-up looked serious, and in the first few minutes it quickly became apparent that the local boys meant business.

Australian-born James Gallagher from Adelaide notched the first score of the game before Ireland fired into the lead with goals from Benny Coulter, Paddy Bradley and Killian Young. The visitors led by 3–6 to 1–9 at half time, and that despite some bizarre yet hilarious efforts at goal (namely an attempted bicycle kick from Kieran Donaghy). Apparently, there had been a private wager for anyone who could score something spectacular. These boys were having fun. NSW fought back, thanks to a personal haul of 1–6 from NSW's own Kerry star Kevin Lynch, and it was a point from the Castleisland man at the death that saw honours finish even. NSW 3–17, Ireland 6–8, just for the record. Decent game it was, too.

After the final whistle, fans young and old swarmed the field as players obliged with autographs and posed for photos. If you're trying to persuade an Aussie youngster to take up Gaelic football, or indeed keep playing Gaelic football, there's no better tonic than sticking him in a picture alongside a grinning Kieran Donaghy. Realise it or not, the guy is an icon – the best barometer has always been excited 12 year olds! Indeed, Donaghy was in high demand, more so than any other player after the final whistle. The fellow just never seemed to stop smiling. Talk around the Aussie campfires in the week between the first and second Tests had been all about his interview with Kennelly on the field at Subiaco in Perth after the first game. Kennelly, who had been acting as an onfield reporter for Channel Seven, had cornered Donaghy for a post-match chat. The two had launched into a conversation in what can only be described as 'Kerry English'. The punchline had been the utterly bewildered looks on the faces of the Australian presenters after Tadhg had thrown it back to the studio. *Gi hiontach.*

After the game, the team were supposed to be heading back to the Four Seasons hotel in the city for a post-match banquet with the local GAA honchos. Only about four or five of them showed up, though the entire NSW team were sitting around eating their dinner. This was their All-Ireland. They wouldn't be long in following the Irish team up to PJ O'Brien's across the road, though. The senior Irish team figures had made it their business to be at the function, and after the grub was polished off I strolled across the room to a table in the corner. Around it were Seán Cavanagh, Seán Kelly and Colm Begley. Three peas in a pod, nattering away and enjoying the trip. For Begley, though, it had been a very rough few weeks.

While the International Rules series had been kicking into high gear, the Laois man had learned that he was being de-listed by the Brisbane Lions. After an injury-riddled season, he had lost his place in the senior team right at the end of the year to Mayo starlet Pearce Hanley. It had seemed a fairly innocuous transition at the time and none of us had thought much of it. At season's end, the Lions' head coach and chief Begley fan, Leigh Matthews, had been replaced in the boss's chair by former player Michael Voss. Voss, it seemed, had no room in his plans for Begley. All this had happened in the throes of the International Rules series and, in fairness to Begley, it might have been for the best that he had been left with little or no time to ponder the uncertainty of his professional future. Sitting around the table, he seemed incredibly upbeat about his prospects. He'd played 29 matches in the AFL and was widely regarded as one of the better prospects out there. He genuinely didn't seem at all worried. Thankfully, he didn't need to be. A few weeks later he was snapped up by St Kilda, so would soon be busy setting up a new home in Melbourne.

The official aspects of the function had been long wrapped up as the players began their exodus to PJ's. The Irish team had set up base upstairs in the popular Sydney city venue, and licensee Fergal McCauley was grinning from ear to ear as I rolled in. I'd only seen him this happy twice before – the first time in this exact same spot, rubbing my head with glee as Tyrone wiped the floor with Dublin in the All-Ireland quarter-final, and the second when he had been running around looking for Tadhg Kennelly in Madam De Biers that September Sunday. He was busy racing around the bar, keeping everyone in beer, as I rolled up to say hello. But in the corner of my eye I'd spotted a second big smiley head – that of Kennelly. He and Begley were loving having the Irish boys in town, and the Kerryman in particular had been pulling out all the stops to make sure they were all enjoying themselves. After landing in from Melbourne the night before with the team, Tadhg had rocked up to a busy city nightclub and waltzed to the front of the queue. Kennelly plus 22, please. No wuckin furries, mate. Legend.

The Irish team were planning a heavy night ahead, now that their duties were done. It had been a busy few weeks for them and it was only now that the grind of training and games – which the Kerry and Tyrone boys in particular had been at non-stop for at least 11 months or more – was coming to an end. They weren't due to fly back to Ireland until the Thursday, and with plans to hit the Melbourne Cup in Flemington on the Tuesday, it was set to be a mighty session. One member of the squad who wouldn't be joining in on all that fun, however, was Wicklow's Leighton Glynn. The Rathnew man was flying home the following morning ahead of his hurling club Glenealy's county senior final replay against Carnew. He'd be missing the guts of the craic, sure, but he didn't care. That wasn't what he lived and died for. He would tell me – and it was so hard not to believe – that he was only too delighted to be getting the chance to do his bit for his club. Glynn had arguably been Ireland's best player in the International Rules series. He had certainly won fans in Australia, and a huge posse of local kids would be waiting to welcome him home when he arrived in Rathnew on the Wednesday. A nicer fella you couldn't hope to meet. Glenealy would go on to win the Wicklow title. Just desserts for those who've finished their veggies.

The rest of the Irish team eventually filtered out of PJ's and on to pastures greener, but with work in the morning I decided to head for home. It felt like an ending. The GAA season in Ireland, NSW and even America had all finally come to an end. This was where my GAA worldwide journey would finally finish. I'd been around the world and back again. It had to end somewhere.

FRIDAY, 27 FEBRUARY 2009 – DEADLINE DAY

It was now 20 months on since I had first come up with the concept of racing around the planet from one GAA club to the next. It had been quite the adventure and I'd learned a lot. My whole world view had been forever altered. Some things never change, though. Kilkenny were still the All-Ireland hurling champions, for example. At senior, under-21 and minor. Portumna had just won through to another All-Ireland club final, and Cushendall had been beaten for the sixth consecutive year in a semi-final. The Cork hurling team were on strike – again – while Kilmacud Crokes and Crossmaglen were set to duke it out in the club football final a few weeks later. Crossmaglen were after their fifth title and Crokes their second. There'd be a lot of familiar faces making the trip to Croke Park on St Patrick's Day.

The Christmas months had been unusually quiet on the inter-county front. All of a sudden the county teams were on a serious hiatus. Under new rules they weren't allowed to train together during November and December, and so there had been very little to report outside of the club championships. GAA land was in hibernation in Ireland, but outside of Europe the GAA turbine never stops turning.

In December in San Francisco, the All Stars tour had been a great success. A massive highlight had obviously been the opening of the Treasure Island facility, now christened Páirc na nGael.

Most of the GAA dignitaries in North America had shown up for the event, as the continental conference was also being held that same week. Nickey Brennan was there to dedicate the new facility, but a week later they also had Irish president Mary McAleese in town to dedicate the junior field – now called Páirc na nÓg.

It was all go that month in the Bay Area, but while presidential figures were dedicating sports grounds and attending functions Liam Reidy had been squirrelling away on a project of his own. A few weeks earlier he had organised and participated in the first-ever colleges hurling match in North America. The University of California in Berkeley, where Reidy was studying for a PhD, had taken on their local school rivals, Stanford. Amazingly, only three Irish lads had played in the game. Reidy from Broadford in Limerick and Conor Molumby from Dublin had lined out for Berkeley, while a Tipperary man named Eoin Buckley had togged for Stanford.

The Berkeley team had obviously come about off the back of the efforts of Reidy, but the Stanford side was the brainchild of an Irish-American named John Mulrow. He, along with Buckley, had been working hard all year and they were turning heads on campus. Apparently, at a training session one day, visiting former Pakistani President Pervez Musharraf had slowed down his passing motorcade to take a look at the bizarre spectacle. In the end, though, it was the University of California's Bears who came out on top, thanks to a last-minute point. They hope the game will catch on and that other Californian universities will pick it up, and they might someday start an inter-varsity league. More power to them.

Back in Sydney, though, things had really changed. Tyrone minor star Kyle Coney had come to NSW after signing with the Sydney Swans. He'd been reportedly settling in quite well, seemed to be enjoying training and was living with Tadhg Kennelly and Brendan Murphy in Tadhg's house on Bondi. By all accounts, he appeared to be comfy in his new career in the AFL. He went home for Christmas to his friends and family after six weeks in Sydney – and never came back.

At one point in December, there were three Irishmen at the Swans. Just a few weeks later, Murphy was the only one left. Coney had taken his ball and gone home, much to everyone's surprise (especially the Swans, who had told me they'd learned of Coney's defection in the Irish newspapers), and Tadhg Kennelly had just announced his retirement from professional football. It hadn't been a major surprise, but he was ducking out a year early on his contract, so it was a case of believing it when seen. On 29 January, he announced his final call at a press conference in the SCG. It was a sad affair. Everyone in Sydney was going to miss him. But everyone understood.

It was a tough decision, the toughest of his life, he'd say. But Tadhg had had an air of genuine contentment as he addressed the assembled media at the SCG. He was there to announce a decision he'd been putting off for two years. He was saying farewell to his illustrious AFL career and opening a new chapter in his life. After almost a decade in Australia, he was calling it a day with the Swans and heading home to play football.

With the final question answered, he'd taken a look around, and a deep intake of breath. He'd cheerily greeted all who approached. Taking it all in. This was a giant leap and he knew it. AFL was all he'd known his entire adult life. He knew this was his final press conference in a Swans shirt, but he didn't have the look of a man who'd just lost an old friend. Instead he seemed like a man happy with his lot. Ready to take on a new challenge. Ready to be who he was born to be in the eyes of many Kerry football people. The Prodigal Son was on his way home at last.

'It was a very tough decision. I obviously had to think long and hard about it. Telling the guys in the dressing-room was probably one of the hardest things I've ever had to do in my life. I spent ten years out here and it was the best ten years of my life,' he told me before he left for Ireland. 'I'm really going to miss the boys. I've built up some great relationships in my time here, so that's going to be tough. I'm really going to miss Australia; it's my home. I love this country. I'm lucky in that I have two homes, in a sense.'

The reasons were simple. They were all about his family. He wanted to go home to his mother, his friends, his former life. He wanted to get back what he'd given up to come to Australia. He wanted to do what his father – the late, great Tim – had done. He knew that one more season with the Swans, one more injury, one more mistimed tackle, and not only would his AFL career be over but also any dream of ever pulling on the green and gold of the Kingdom. It just simply wasn't worth the risk.

'I've been away from my family a long time now and I've been through a lot. That was one of the reasons. But the other reason was obviously the football. I want to play for Kerry, I want to follow in my father's footsteps and win an All-Ireland.

'I grew up idolising my father. I felt that if I played another year of AFL that my body wouldn't be able to go through going home and playing Gaelic football.

'I'd be half the player, if I stayed. It would always be in the back of my mind that I might get injured and that I wouldn't be able to go home and play football.'

It had all started to go wrong two years earlier when the injuries began taking their toll. Tadhg reckoned he'd been really lucky up until then, but after 24 months on physios' benches, in surgical theatres and having his shoulder popped back in on a regular basis, it was beginning to get a bit much. Frustrating wasn't even the word. He'd actually suffered two sports hernia injuries in the last two years alone, aside from the chronic groin problems, knee injuries and shoulder dislocations. He wondered if there'd be anything left of him to play for Kerry. Only one way to find out.

His had been a glorious career. His Hall of Fame tagline will forever be 'First Irishman to win a Premiership' – but to sum up his groundbreaking decade of work in just six words would be to grossly understate the magnitude of his achievements in Australia, let alone the legacy those achievements have left in their wake Down Under and beyond.

There are eight Irish players on the books of AFL clubs at the time of writing (not including Tadhg). You have to wonder how many of those would be in Australia had Kennelly not opened the door. He admits his career had been a dream. He could never have imagined such success when he first got off the boat ten years ago. 'I had no major career goals in mind when I first came out here. I just wanted to play football and get myself into the senior team. I gave it my best shot and thankfully everything worked out well. I had a great career. Here I am, ten years later.'

He says he'd recommend it to anyone and would 'certainly encourage anyone to give it a go in Australia'. However, he's at a 'different point' in his life to the bright-eyed and bushy-tailed Brian Donnellys and Conor Merediths of this world. For now, that chapter of his life is over. When God closes a door, he opens a window, they say. Kennelly would be possibly the fittest, best-trained, most-qualified man ever to set his sights on making a debut in a senior inter-county football team. We've certainly never seen a rookie of his like before. Remember, folks, he's only out of minor.

'I can't wait to get a hold of a round ball again instead of that awful thing they have over here!' he'd joked. 'At least the round ball hops back to you when you bounce it. Hopefully, the professional training I've had and all I've learned about how to look after my body will be an advantage when I get home. I've been in touch with Jack [Kerry manager Jack O'Connor] and I told him I was thinking of going back. He said, "Right, come on back." I'm not expecting to be treated any different from anyone else. I certainly haven't been guaranteed a place in the squad or anything like that, I'm going to have to work my ass off to get in there. I'm looking forward to getting back and playing with Listowel. To be honest, I'm probably more looking forward to playing with Listowel than anything else. Getting back there and playing with my mates – I can't wait.'

The one man left behind in all these defections was Murphy. 'I told Brendan a while ago that I was thinking about it, but I only made the decision when I was talking to Roosy [Swans coach Paul

Roos]. It's going to be tough on Brendan, but he'll find his own feet. He'll get set up in his own lifestyle and maybe this could be a good thing for him to get out of my shadow.'

A lot of people were wondering just what Kennelly was going to do with himself after he got home. With the family pub sold on, we wondered what career options might be open to a 27-year-old former professional football player in a recession. Nine-to-five in the depths of a dirty Irish winter might take some getting used to. Tadhg admitted with a big grin that it's 'probably not the best time to be going home economically', but that he had little to worry about. Aussie Rules had been kind to him. And to his bank balance. Still, though, you need something to pass the long lonely hours. 'I'll have to get myself a job. I'm unemployed at the moment and I'll have to do something, but I suppose I'll figure that out as I go. I'm really not worried about that side of things at all. I've done well out of the game, I'd be the first one to tell you that. It's not as if I'm going to be living on the side of the street or anything like that.'

One woman delighted to see him return was his mother, Nuala. It had been a tough few years for the Listowel woman after the loss of Tadhg's father Tim, but after ten years on the other side of the world her son was finally on his way home. 'I told her what I was thinking and she was a bit emotional about it. But, you know, to be honest I don't think she'll quite believe it until I walk off the plane.'

It seems unlikely that this will be the last Sydney will see of the Kerryman. If he were to do the unthinkable and win an All-Ireland with Kerry in his first year, would he consider coming back to Sydney and rekindling his Swans career? 'I'm not going to close the door on anything.' There's plenty of room left in this story for more than one new chapter.

Tadhg had been the spiritual leader of the Irish lads Down Under. With him gone, Setanta Ó hAilpín had become the elder statesman. And he was having a month he'd rather forget. He'd struggled the previous few years at his club, Carlton. This was his final contracted season in Melbourne and he knew it was now or never. He had to have a big year. In the end, he was lucky to have any sort of year at all. A crazy incident in an intra-club game in Melbourne nearly ended his career. A spat with teammate Cameron Cloke had escalated into something more serious. He'd lost the rag, punched Cloke and tapped him with his foot as his body lay motionless on the turf. Of course, Murphy's Law, the whole thing had been caught on film. The outcry from the Melbourne media was deafening. They'd never really liked him and smelled blood in the water. They were out to finish him.

Within hours of his 'brain snap', the media had branded Ó hAilpín 'a bad sport' as well as 'a bad influence' who had 'brought shame and despair' into the game and who was guilty of 'nothing short of assault'. By Friday evening on 6 February, Setanta's AFL epitaph had been written and the sound of sharpening knives could be heard all around the Yarra. Torches were being lit and pitchforks raised. John Ralph wrote in the *Herald Sun*: 'The problem for Ó hAilpín is that he has form, and plenty of it. At Carlton, Ó hAilpín is known for two characteristics: a thick Irish brogue littered with profanities, and for being an angry young man in a hurry. At best Ó hAilpín is a fourth-choice ruckman and a fifth-choice tall defender. Now he looks almost certain to join his brother and Sydney's Irish star Tadhg Kennelly back in the homeland with his last act in the navy blue being one that brought shame and despair.'

Ouch. I wondered just how long Mr Ralph had been keeping his powder dry on that one. It wasn't just him, though. There was a queue for this particular public hanging.

Ralph's *Herald Sun* colleague Robyn Riley added, 'Within hours of video footage of the assault going online on the *Herald Sun* webpage, more than 10,000 readers had viewed it. Some would have been children.' Oh dear Lord, won't somebody please think of the children.

But back in your respective boxes, John and Robyn. This ain't amateur hour. We want to see real outrage here, people. Think lollipop thief meets puppy-drowner. Take it away, Mr Patrick Smith of *The Australian*. 'While attacking someone's anus is not unheard of in rugby league, Ó hAilpín's boot up the backside of prostrate Cameron Cloke was nothing short of assault. Carlton really just ought to sack Ó hAilpín.' Much better.

Luckily, Carlton weren't going to be influenced by such unqualified outrage. They made up their own minds. He made a mistake, it shouldn't have happened, it had been dealt with. The AFL dished out their punishment and even victim Cloke said it was water under the bridge. Within days, everyone had got the whole thing out of their systems. The Melbourne media had even changed their tune. Their leader on displays of righteous indignation, the migraine-inducing Mike Sheahan, even climbed down from atop his high horse long enough to admit some culpability in the anti-Setanta campaign. 'Ó hAilpín will survive at Carlton, and we're pleased. He has invested a huge amount of time, energy and emotion into his AFL dream. He deserves to see out his contract. Obviously, we overreacted on Friday. Grossly. All of us. Setanta Ó hAilpín's four-match suspension on charges of striking and kicking tells us so.'

Hang on, though. There's still room for a completely unnecessary token Irish reference about the man he has colourfully christened 'Setantrum'. 'Drop a certain two letters out of his first name and what do you get? Santa. It was Christmas and a birthday in one for Ó hAilpín [the AFL sanction of a four-game cup suspension]. He has a four-leaf clover in his bag of tricks, the big Irishman.' Be gosh and begorrah, Mike, that's some mighty fine sorry-making.

Not once in all this did anyone think to ask what had driven Setanta to it. Of course, we're not saying anything could justify the attack on Cloke, but you'd think someone might have at least asked the question. One rational voice did stick its head out amidst the madness of the 'Setantagate' scandal.

'The Setanta Ó hAilpín punch has been blown completely out of proportion,' AFL blogger Into the Black wrote. 'Cam Cloke has forgiven the Irishman and just wants to get on with it. Do you know why he has forgiven Setanta? It's because before the players were wrestling, Cam Cloke backhanded Setanta in the throat. So not only has this been blown out of proportion, Cam Cloke is actually at fault. He started it. He should be the one getting suspended. Can you believe that this was the cover page news story of the *Herald Sun*? What? Slow f***ing news day.'

Carlton and the AFL took a similar view. In fact, some were even ready to laugh about the whole thing a few days later. 'At least he beat up a former Collingwood player,' club president Stephen Kernahan joked. Legend.

It was a lot easier to see the funny side with the dust finally beginning to settle. Setanta himself had been all but locked away from the media in the aftermath. It was head down and shoulder-to-the-mill stuff. His entire career was hanging in the balance, but the character he would go on to show was testament to his own battling qualities. When I caught up with him a few months later, he'd put the whole thing pretty much behind him and was enjoying his most successful season ever on the field. He had fought his way back into the starting line-up at Carlton and had played his 50th Premiership game for the club after what had begun as a nightmare year; he had also lost the companionship of brother Aisake, who had returned home to Ireland after a spell at the Blues.

With the 2009 season more than halfway through, he'd kicked a career-high four goals against Fremantle in Perth. It was all coming together again. The most triumphant stories often emerge from the greatest of adversity and, having come through the mill, Setanta had grown exponentially from his experiences. 'In life, you get your ups and downs, and obviously this year didn't start the way I would have liked,' Setanta recalled philosophically. 'It was more frustration than anything. I'd finally found out what had been causing all my injury problems. I had two blocked arteries in my legs. Back in November I'd had the operation to solve that and I was really behind the eight ball coming back. When I returned, I was really unfit and there was a real build-up of frustration there.

There's heaps of ways you could look at it [the incident], but what I did at the end with the kick wasn't on at all. Not only in this game, but it wouldn't have been on in GAA. But after that I just told myself that I'd put the head down and the bum up and work as hard as I could. I've done my time now and I'd like to think that if a situation like that arose again I wouldn't react the same way. I've moved on since then and, to be honest, I just want to put the whole thing behind me.'

A major low point had come with the departure of his brother. His younger sibling had been a crutch for Setanta in a city so far from home. With the sky falling, he found himself all alone in Melbourne.

'Yeah, I definitely really missed Aisake when he left. He's only two years younger than me and, growing up, we did everything together. We went to school together, we trained together and we would have played in most teams together. So not only was he my brother, he was also a good friend. To have him around when things weren't going well used to be great. We could bounce off one another. When he left, a part of me felt really sad because he was the only family I had out here. It was pretty disappointing and a bit sad for me, but I suppose that's life. He's moving on to bigger and better things.'

When Setanta first arrived in Australia, Kennelly had been a big inspiration to him. He even changed his guernsey number to 17, jointly in honour of Kennelly and of 17 March, St Patrick's Day. He stays in regular contact with the now-departed Listowel man, who moved home to play with Kerry, but the role of father figure had now fallen back on Setanta's ample shoulders with the arrival of two of Carlton's new recruits, Zach Tuohy from Laois and fellow Corkman Ciaran Sheehan. 'I ring Tadhg the odd time. I talk to him about football and about how he's going and how I'm going. I'd be watching him on Setanta Sports and he watches my games any chance he gets. But it's great to stay in touch.'

Setanta had watched the Cork v. Galway All-Ireland hurling

qualifier at his home in Melbourne with the two Irish recruits just before I'd caught up with him.

It's one of those things you can never really get away from, no matter how hard you try. He'll always be a Corkman – and a hurling man, to boot – and watching his two brothers tog out for the Rebels in the championship cauldron is always going to be tough to stomach when you're on the other side of the planet. 'Yeah, that's when you really feel the homesickness. Watching the game was tough. Having been there myself and having played in championship games like that, that's when you really start to feel homesick. Having Seán Óg and Aisake out there, all I wanted to do was go out and play with my two brothers. Having them both there playing for Cork, it gets a bit sad at times looking at them. But I suppose that's life, ya know.'

Despite all his trials and tribulations in 2009, Setanta has emerged with a positive outlook – although he was still prone to the odd bizarre injury. 'I did my hammy there recently. I got a knee in the back and that swelled up and bled into my hamstring. It's not the sort of injury you'd exactly be used to, but that's the game and you've just got to get on with it. I was just starting to play a bit of consistent footy, so it was disappointing in that way, with the timing of it. But I can't tell the future. Things are going to happen and you're going to get injured. You've just got to get on with it and try to get it right again.'

On a personal note, it had been a great year for him. One milestone he never thought he'd reach was that of playing 50 games. In reaching that goal, he'd become just the fourth Irishman to do so, joining Kennelly, Sean Wight and Jim Stynes. Setanta says the achievement was 'something a bit special for myself', but the real priority for him was team honours. As we got to talking of finals and play-offs, the topic of a potential medal soon reared its head. Pushed as to whether a Premiership medal or an All-Ireland would mean more to him, you begin to realise that he's only 26 years old and has actually spent almost all of his adult life playing Aussie Rules in Melbourne. So, has the childhood dream of lifting Liam or Sam been replaced by something he's worked towards for every single day of his entire professional adult life?

'Both are equal in my mind, I think. Playing hurling growing up since I was five years old, and training and playing with Na Piarsaigh, all I ever wanted to do was to wear the Cork jersey. Having been there myself, and playing in a losing All-Ireland final, it's always been a burning ambition of mine to win an All-Ireland. But moving over here to play football, the Premiership medal is the big thing. Playing a game I didn't grow up with, to win a Premiership medal and emulate Tadhg, that would be the ultimate for me, I think. But who knows? Hopefully some day I could win both. I hold both in very high regard. Only a few people on this earth get the chance to play in Grand Finals or All-Ireland finals, and to win one is very special. To be able to look back on your career when it's all said and done and be able to say you've won either would be something very special.'

It was great to see Setanta rise up from the most testing time of his life, but his tale was only one of a growing Irish storybook Down Under. It used to be the case that you followed either Kennelly's Swans, Marty Clarke's Collingwood, Setanta's Carlton or Colm Begley's Brisbane Lions. That has all changed. There were new kids in town.

Begley, first of all, had moved to St Kilda and had just a few weeks previously made his debut. Mayo's Pearce Hanley was now the go-to guy in Brisbane. In Adelaide, Brian Donnelly of Louth was making great strides – 'better than banging nails back home', he'd colourfully stated in his first few weeks in Oz – while Longford teenager Michael Quinn had just started his first game for the Essendon Bombers in the pre-season NAB Cup. Begley's fellow Laois man Conor Meredith was settling into life at the North Melbourne Kangaroos, while Clarke and Armagh youngster Kevin Dyas were preparing for the year ahead at Collingwood. Dyas was one of the brightest Irish prospects, but his 2008 had been cut tragically short by a bad hamstring injury. After a wonderful start to his time with the Magpies, which had club officials raving, Dyas's injury had ended his season. He had been out of action for the past seven months, but now that he was on the verge of regaining full fitness he hoped that it wouldn't be long before he donned the black-and-white stripes of the Melbourne club again. The 21 year old from Dromintee had come through that particular challenge with flying colours and he was ready to make an impact.

Back in Sydney, Brendan Murphy had trained himself to the Setanta Ó hAilpín way of thinking. He was alone in the city and he knew he needed to make the most of it. He had to make an impact this season. It was now or never. After a relaxing three weeks at home in Carlow over Christmas, in which he even got a couple of run-outs with his club, Rathvilly, Murphy was back in the groove. An ankle injury had slowed him down a little and had cost him his place in the NAB Cup squad, but he was happy with his progress and delighted to be back into his now familiar routine. After a season that had taken him to the brink of a senior debut in 2008, he had set his sights on one main goal for the year ahead – his maiden bow in the AFL as a first-team Swans player. Anything short of that would be a failure in the eyes of the talented giant.

'The goal is definitely to try to play first-team football this year. I really want to try and get a few games in the first team, and if I haven't achieved that by the end of the season I'll consider the year as having been a failure for me. I've had long enough to settle in, it's business time now.'

Murphy's progress had been interrupted somewhat by leg problems in 2008. The rush to put on the weight he knew he needed to compete for a place in the first team, as well as to survive in the rough physical world of the AFL, had caused an undesired reaction in the rest of his body. Shin splints and muscular problems duly followed.

'I'm over that now, thank God. What happened was that I put on ten kilos too early last year and I ended up weighing too much. I ended up straining my groin, and then my shins started at me, and I couldn't even train half the time. But I managed to drop back a few kilos and I'm feeling fine now. I'm fully fit for the year ahead and I'm really looking forward to it.'

Before heading home for the Christmas break, Murphy had been training alongside Tyrone star Coney, but it wasn't until Murphy returned to Sydney that he heard of Coney's decision not to come back. 'I didn't know a thing about it. He told me he was coming back when I was talking to him before Christmas, so I don't know what's happening. I didn't actually hear about it until I got back to Sydney. I'd been on to him all right when I was at home, but I didn't get a reply from him. It was a big shock to me. I'm sure he'll have a great career and all that with Tyrone. I just hope he doesn't end up regretting it. We were training together and he was going well. He was kicking really well and he said he was enjoying it, so I don't know what happened. I think he said he realised how much he missed home.'

The Coney situation is still up in the air, but by the end of the 2009 season there wouldn't be a single Irishman left at the Swans, as Murphy called it a day. There were, however, more than a few Irish youngsters forging paths in Brisbane, Adelaide and Melbourne. And doing very, very well for themselves, by all accounts. A special mention goes to Longford teenager Michael Quinn at the Essendon Bombers, who broke into the first team almost straight away. I'll certainly be keeping tabs on his progress as his star continues to rise Down Under.

On a personal level, this little journey of mine had to end somewhere. And this was it. Looking back over the previous year and a half, it really had been quite an amazing experience. I'd learned so much on my travels, but even after all the thousands of miles I'd covered I was left with one recurring thought: I could do another lap of the globe, from GAA club to GAA club, without hitting any of the places I'd already been to. As I've said before, I'd only scratched the surface.

GAA CLUBS OF THE WORLD OUTSIDE EUROPE: CONTACT LIST

SOUTH AMERICA

Hurling Club of Buenos Aires (Argentina):
Daithi Ó Caoimh admin@hurling-club.com.ar

ASIA

Asian County Board
Chairman:
Paraic McGrath (Singapore) pmcgrath@tullettprebon.com.sg
Vice-Chairman:
Mick McCannon (Taiwan) mccannon@yahoo.co.uk
Treasurer:
Michael Shannon (Beijing) michael.shannon@lionbridge.com
PRO:
Peter Ryan (Singapore) peter.ryan@asef.org

CLUBS

Abu Dhabi Na Fianna (United Arab Emirates):
James Ryan james.ryan@hct.ac.ae
Bahrain GAA:
Dermot Wallis dermot.wallis@aramco.com
Bangkok Thai GAAs (Thailand):
John Campbell gaathailand@yahoo.com
Beijing GAA (China):
Aoife O'Loughlin beijinggaa@yahoo.com
Clan na hOman (Oman):
Steve O'Connor steve@muscatdutyfree.com

Dalian Wolfhounds (China):
Mikey Farrelly mikeyfarrelly@gmail.com
Dubai Celts (United Arab Emirates):
Daithí Hanley david.leonard.hanley@citi.com
Hong Kong GAA (China):
Shane Harmon shane.harmon@gmail.com
Japan GAA:
Ruairi Hatchell ruairijapan@gmail.com
Kansai GAA (Japan):
Fergus O'Dwyer kansaigaa@gmail.com
Orang Éire (Malaysia):
Eoin Duggan eoin.duggan@dfa.ie
Penang Pumas (Malaysia):
Dr Paddy Kiernan info@penang-irish-association.com
Seoul Gaels (South Korea):
Kevin Tobin seoulgaels@gmail.com
Shanghai Saints and Sirens (China):
Mick MacCannon contact@shanghaigaelic.com
Shenzhen Celts (China):
Louise Weste info@shenzhencelts.com
Singapore Gaelic Lions:
Peter Ryan peter.ryan@asef.org
Taiwan Celts:
Barry Cahill cahill_barry@yahoo.com
Viet Celts (Vietnam):
Sean Hoy sean.hoy@dfa.ie

AUSTRALASIA

Australasian County Board
Chairman:
Seamus Sullivan (Brisbane) seamus@idealelectrical.com.au
Secretary:
Gerard Roe (Alice Springs) gerardro@bigpond.net.au

BOARDS

Auckland GAA (New Zealand):
Liam O'Keeffe liam.okeeffe@leightonworks.co.nz
Fiji GAA:
Gerald Lohan geraldlohan8@hotmail.com

CONTACT LIST

New South Wales GAA (Sydney):
Ned Sheehy sheehy@iinet.net.au
Queensland GAA (Brisbane):
Theresa Robinson theresarobinson@optusnet.com.au
South Australia GAA (Adelaide):
Norm Murphy normmurphy@ozemail.com.au
Tasmania GAA:
Barbara Middleton gaelicfootballtas@gmail.com
Victoria GAA (Melbourne):
Pauline McIntyre pmcintyre@iinet.net.au
Wellington GAA (New Zealand):
Justin McDermott Justin.McDermott@fish.govt.nz
Western Australia GAA (Perth):
Sean O'Casey socasey@rwvp.com.au

CLUBS

NEW ZEALAND
Auckland
Celtic:
Barry Brennan bandsbrennan@xtra.co.nz
Gaels:
Jimmy Connolly dancingkiwi@xtra.co.nz
Harps:
Mick O'Malley momalley@steinhoff.com.au
Rangers:
Mike Fox mikef@reoco.co.nz

Wellington
Black Harps:
Tony Gormley gormleygang@xtra.co.nz
Molly Malones:
Donal Kavanagh donal.kavanagh@seaworks.co.nz

FIJI
Fiji GAA:
Gerald Lohan geraldlohan8@hotmail.com

AUSTRALIA

New South Wales

Central Coast:
Steve Carey info@thecoastgaa.com
Clan na Gael:
Martina O'Brien martina.obrien@ambition.com.au
Cormac McAnallen's:
Liam O'Hara info@cormacmcanallensgac.com.au
Craobh Pádraig:
Shane O'Brien cppats@gmail.com
Michael Cusack's:
Yvonne Rooney roo.yvonne@gmail.com
Penrith Gaels:
Gerry Roper caoradubh@aol.com
Sydney Shamrocks Hurling Club:
Declan Maher decandciara@gmail.com
University of Wollongong Fighting Leprechauns:
Lee Murray lmurray@uow.edu.au
Young Ireland's:
Seamus Collins collins_seamus@emc.com

Queensland

Easts:
Dov Hirst dovh@optusnet.com.au
Harps:
Leith Poulsen goldiey73@hotmail.com
John Mitchels:
Vinnie Campbell johnmitchels@yahoo.com.au
Queensland Hurling and Camogie:
Donie Whelan doniewhelan@hotmail.com
Sarsfields:
Theresa Robinson mactessa@hotmail.com
Shamrocks:
James Marshall jamesm@myself.com
Souths:
Vanessa Martens southsgaa@hotmail.com

CONTACT LIST

South Australia

Angry Leprechauns:
Chris Carey ccarey@hotmail.com
Eastern Gaels:
Jamie Phillips PHILJL003@students.unisa.edu.au
Flinders O'Neills:
Paddy McGuinness paddymac1@bigpond.com
Irish Australians:
Michael Emmett emmettmj@hotmail.com
Irwin Allstars:
Nic Pearson nicpearson@hassell.com.au
Jets:
James Puopolo jdpuopolo@hotmail.com
Na Fianna:
Mick Lawlor edelandmick@intermode.on.net
Onkaparinga:
Des Packer dpa43489@bigpond.net.au
Red Lions:
Henry McGregor redlionsgfc@hotmail.com
Shenanigans:
Matt Gibbs mgibbs@civeng.adelaide.edu.au
St Brendan's:
Rob Barrachina rob_barra@hotmail.com
University of South Australia:
Julie Smith juliesmith@andersons.com.au
Western Ireland:
David Floreani flogga9@hotmail.com

Tasmania

Tasmania GAA:
Marie Keating mariekkcc@yahoo.co.uk

Victoria

Garryowen:
Alysha Courtney garryowen@garryowengac.com.au
Grace O'Malley's:
Caz Daly cazdaly14@hotmail.com
Melbourne Shamrocks:
Clodagh McIntyre clodaghmcintyre@hotmail.com

Pádraig Pearse's:
Jane Murphy janemurphy@reach.org.au
Sinn Féin:
Dearne Leonard dearne.leonard@gmail.com
St Kevin's:
Pat Gavin pat@del-phi.com.au
Victoria Camogie:
Andrea Keane andrea.keane76@gmail.com
Wolfe Tones:
Ciaran Mohan cmohan@wolfetones.net

Western Australia
Coastal Breakers:
Jay Williamson jacqualine.williamson@asgardwealthsolutions.com.au
Greenswood GFC:
Vaughan Castine vaughan@castinet.com.au
Morley Gaels:
Steven Smolders balmoralpools@optusnet.com.au
Southern Districts:
Lucy Gallop lgallop@westernpacific.com.au
St Finnbarr's:
Keiron Burke paulankeiron@optusnet.com.au
WA Camogie:
Jennie Codd www.gaawa.org.au
Western Shamrocks:
John Lehane johnog62@hotmail.com

CANADA
Canadian County Board
Chairman:
Brian Farmer psc@powerscreencanada.com
Secretary:
John O'Flynn canadagaa@gmail.com

BOARDS
Toronto Divisional Board:
Gabriel Hurl ghurl@cm2r.com
Western Canada Divisional Board:
Calum Bonnington calumb@shaw.ca

CLUBS

Toronto Divisional Board

Brampton Roger Casements:
Erin Higgins brc_gaelicfootball@hotmail.com
Durham Robert Emmets:
Brendan O'Neill info@durhamgfc.com
Michael Cusack's Ladies' Football Club:
Danielle Hurst irishgal_loves_tigger@hotmail.com
Montreal Shamrocks:
Michael Martin montrealshamrocksgaa@gmail.com
Ottawa Gaels:
Daphne Ballard info@ottawagaels.ca
St Mike's:
Ronan Matthews st_mikesgaa@hotmail.com
St Pat's Canadians:
Sean Morley sean_morley@rogers.com
St Vincent's:
Ken Ray ken_ray23@hotmail.com
Toronto Gaels:
Greg Callan gcallan@hotmail.com

Western Canada Divisional Board

Calgary Chieftains:
Adrian Lagan laganadrian@yahoo.co.uk
Edmonton Wolfe Tones:
Kim Budd kimberley.budd@shaw.ca
Vancouver Irish:
Marcus Treacy info@issvancouver.com

CAYMAN ISLANDS

CLUBS

Cayman Islands GAA Club:
Howard Byrne howard.byrne@gmail.com

UNITED STATES OF AMERICA

North American County Board

Chairman:
Joe Lydon joelydon@aol.com
Secretary:
Liam Moloney liamamoloney@aol.com
Vice-Chairman:
Paul McCarthy philagaa@comcast.net
PRO:
Eamonn Kelly eamonnkelly@comcast.net

New York County Board

Chairman:
Larry McCarthy mccartla@shu.edu
Secretary:
Liam Bermingham lbermingha@aol.com
Registrar:
Joan Henchy henchy4@optusonline.net

North American County Board: Divisions

Central Division (Chicago):
Harry Costelloe hcostel@sbcglobal.net
Mid Atlantic Division (Washington DC):
Niall Dempsey secretary@wdcgaels.com
Midwest Division (Cleveland):
David Slevin dslevin@radio.fm
Northeast Division (all Boston):
Sharon O'Brien secretary@bostongaa.org
Northwest Division (Seattle):
Marjorie Friedman freidmarj@gmail.com
Philadelphia Division:
Paul McCarthy philagaa@comcast.net
Southeast Division (Atlanta):
Sharon McAleer zoo0@cdc.gov
Southwestern Division (Denver/LA/San Diego):
Brian White bwhite697@yahoo.com
Western Division (all San Francisco):
Liam Reidy lreidy@berkeley.edu

CLUBS

Central Division

Cú Chulainn's Hurling Club (Chicago):
Martin Redmond katsmeow12002@yahoo.com
Erin Rovers Ladies' Football Club (Chicago):
Kerry McKinnis kerrymckinnis@yahoo.com
Harry Boland's (Chicago):
Colm Moore mike@premierophthalmic.com
Indianapolis Irish Hurling Club (Indiana):
Jim Kelly greenwoodkelly_s@hotmail.com
John McBride's (Chicago):
Bernadette Byrne johnmcbridesgfc@msn.com
Limerick Hurling Club (Chicago):
Paul Reynolds eirecamogie13@aol.com
Milwaukee Hurling and Camogie Club (Wisconsin):
Matt Larsen get_rad@yahoo.com
Pádraig Pearse's GFC (Chicago):
Fiona Murray fionamurray16@hotmail.com
Parnells (Chicago):
John Rafter chicagoparnells_sec@hotmail.com
Patriots (Chicago):
Sean Moran chicagopatriots@gmail.com
St Brendan's (Chicago):
Amy Coen drewsa27@hotmail.com
St Brigid's Ladies' Football Club (Chicago):
Laura Mitchell mitchbing@hotmail.com
St Louis Football and Hurling Club (Missouri):
Joe Abkemeier jabkemeier@yahoo.com
St Mary's Camogie Club (Chicago):
Nuala Kerlin nualakerlin@yahoo.co.uk
Twin Cities Robert Emmett's (Minnesota):
Adam Coolong adam.coolong@comcast.net
Wolfe Tones (Chicago):
John Devitt jdevitt@sbcglobal.net

Mid Atlantic Division

Baltimore GAA (Maryland):
Lucy Clerkin lucy_clerkin@hotmail.com

Mason-Dixon GAA (Maryland):
Katrina Milligan dflyenvironmental@gmail.com
Washington DC GAA:
Niall Dempsey secretary@wdcgaels.com

Midwest Division

Buffalo Fenians (New York):
David Slevin dslevin@radio.fm
Cleveland St Jarlath's (Ohio):
Jim Coyne jim.coyne.b@bayer.com
Cleveland St Patrick's (Ohio):
Mike Wade mwade12@hotmail.com
Detroit St Anne's (Michigan):
Mary Murray cartyday@aol.com
Detroit Wolfe Tones (Michigan):
Danny McCann dannymccann@fastmail.fm
Pittsburgh Banshees (Pennsylvania):
John Young younger14@hotmail.com
Pittsburgh Celtics (Pennsylvania):
Michael McDonagh mmac_mmac@hotmail.com

Northeast Division

Aidan McAnespie's GFC:
Raymond Brady bradyraymond@yahoo.com
Armagh Notre Dame:
Brian McGrath briandkb@hotmail.com
Boston Celtics:
James Walsh j59jw@aol.com
Boston Shamrocks LGFC:
Eddie Feely dede6@verizon.net
Connemara Gaels:
John Conneely conneelysoup@verizon.net
Cork Football Club:
Lizanne Hourihan lhourihan@pingree.org
Cork Hurling Club:
Dave McSweeney dmcsweeney1@aol.com
Donegal Boston:
John Cunningham donegaljc@yahoo.com
Éire Óg Camogie Club:
Shelly Walsh walsh_shelly@yahoo.co.uk

CONTACT LIST

Fr Tom Burke's Hurling Club:
Michael Moore brencoconst@gmail.com
Galway Football Club:
Peter Nolan info@galwaygfc.com
Galway Hurling Club:
Ann Marie Joyce annmarie_joyce@yahoo.com
Kerry GFC:
Eillis Murphey eillis.murphey@westin.com
Mayo GFC:
Patrick O'Malley frances@crystal-travel.net
New England Celtics:
Liam Fleming Michael_oc_jnr@hotmail.com
Roscommon LGFC:
Nuala McDonnell nualamcdonnell@yahoo.com
St Christopher's GFC:
Paul McCarthy pmccarthy@GCT.com
Tipperary HC:
Bill Kennedy annemkennedy@yahoo.com
Tír na nÓg LGFC:
Courtney Lucas ccarroll.tlucas@gmail.com
Wexford HC:
Peter Nolan hurling04@hotmail.com
Wolfe Tones GFC:
Ray Butler wolfetonesboston@hotmail.com

Northwest Division

Seattle Gaels (Washington):
Scott Gonsar sdgonsar@gmail.com

Philadelphia Division

Brian Boru HC:
Paul McCarthy clonmel99@comcast.net
Éire Óg GFC:
Siobhan Trainor Clonoe@aol.com
Kevin Barry's GFC:
Marty Gallagher kevinbarrysphila@comcast.net
Notre Dame LGFC:
Tara King tara_m_king@merck.com
St Patrick's GFC:
Patrick Bourke rossilly@comcast.net

AROUND THE WORLD IN GAA DAYS

Shamrocks HC:
Brendan McAtamney hurling@philadelphiashamrocks.com
Tyrone GFC:
Peter McDermott pmcdermott@sthe.com
Young Ireland's GFC:
Barry Hassan http://youngirelands.northamerican.gaa.com

Southeast Division (Atlanta)

Atlanta Clan na Gael (Georgia):
Pernille Christensen pernilledk@aol.com
Atlanta Na Fianna LGFC (Georgia):
Erin Whigham thedingo.ateme@yahoo.com
Charlotte James Connolly's GFC (North Carolina):
Kevin Devin kdevin@msn.com
Florida St Patrick's GFC:
Harry Henderson bocaelec@bellsouth.net

Southwestern Division

Austin Celtic Cowboys (Texas):
Pat Doab pat_doab@hotmail.com
Denver Gaels (Colorado):
Cindi Wake lucindawa@hotmail.com
Los Angeles Wild Geese (California):
Ollie Breen ollie@hydrocal.com
Orange County Róisín (California):
Jacquelin Hruby jacquelinhruby@juno.com
Phoenix Gales GFC (Arizona):
Chris Candelaria mrfoyc@yahoo.com
San Diego Na Fianna (California):
Wendy LeVine tigger1996@hotmail.com
San Diego Setanta (California):
Niall Johnston njohnston@mission-advisors.com

Western Division (San Francisco)

Caillini Ceilteach:
Ann McKiernan amckiernan2001@yahoo.com
Celts:
Dan Cotter celtsgfc@gaa.ie
Clan na Gael:
Lisa Connelly lisa61682@yahoo.com

CONTACT LIST

Fog City Harps:
Sarah Kelly sarahkelly53@hotmail.com
Michael Cusack's:
Phillip McCarthy michaelcusacks1989@yahoo.com
Na Fianna:
Liam Fleming secretary@sfnafianna.com
Naomh Padraig GFC:
Lorcan Ryan lorcanryan2@hotmail.com
Saoirse:
Christina Clarke clarkechristina@sbcglobal.net
Sean Treacy's:
H.T. Hughes hthughes@comcast.net
Shamrocks:
Ann McKiernan amckiernan2001@yahoo.com
Shannon Rangers:
Con Brosnan www.bebo.com/shannonrangers
Sons of Boru:
Tom O'Connor webmaster@sonsofboru.com
Ulster:
Kevin McHugh kevinmchugh61@yahoo.com
Young Irelanders/St Brendan's:
Patrick White pwhite@bbri.com

New York County Board – Clubs

Armagh:
Mark McAllister mcallister72@verizon.net
Astoria Gaels:
Eugene Kyne eugene.kyne@structuretone.com
Brooklyn Shamrocks:
Jerry Kiely brendanl@irlsystems.com
Cavan:
Dessie Reilly psheridan19@verizon.net
Cork:
Tom Courtney lberming ha@aol.com
Derry:
Greg McIntyre nmcgovern@cardinalconnect.com
Donegal:
Tommy Lilly donegal3@optonline.net
Down:
Mark Dobbin darner88@hotmail.com

Dublin:
Fergal Mulvanny fergmulv2@aol.com
FDNY:
Brian Quinn mbquinn@hotmail.com
Four Provinces:
Tom Higgins tom_higgins2000@yahoo.com
Galway Hurling:
Ollie Flynn oflynn85@yahoo.com
Kerry:
Joan Henchy henchy4@optonline.net
Leitrim:
Paddy Gormley conor1@optonline.net
Long Island Gaels:
Geraldine O'Brien shamrocker1979@aol.com
Mayo:
Pat Gavin pgavin2@netscape.com
Monaghan:
Seamus Dooley (001) 614 2632474
New Jersey Kilkenny:
Peter Slattery ritaslattery@hotmail.com
Offaly GFC:
John Larkin johnlarkin1971@yahoo.com
Offaly HC:
Alan Gleason johnlarkin1971@yahoo.com
Rangers:
Denis Twomey dtgreenway@aol.com
Rockland:
Kevin Lennon EmmettWoods@verizon.net
Roscommon:
Val McGlynn vmcglynn@aol.com
St Barnaba's:
Eamonn Deane aughawillan@aol.com
St Raymond's:
Pat Ryan pgryan@optonline.net
Sligo:
Larry McCarthy mccartla@shu.edu
Tipperary:
Michael Kennedy michaelk1@optonline.net
Tyrone:
Seamus McNabb mcnabbjames@hotmail.com

ACKNOWLEDGEMENTS

To Pearl for her patience, love, support and tireless encouragement and for putting up with me throughout.

To my family, I owe you everything. Sandra, Seán and Phyllis, who bestowed on me a love for Gaelic Games that is yet to falter, even on the other side of the world, and to Johnny and Matt, who do us all proud every time they pull on the Dublin or Lucan Sarsfields jersey.

To Kevin and Marie and Vinny and Patricia, who are busy building the guts of the 2020 Galway senior teams, to Audrey, who always seems surprised to see me, to Paul, who never lets me forget where I was christened, to the brains of the Kildare operation Karen, and to Laura, Mark and Ava, who gave me something to come home to.

And to my mother Mary, who let me off on this gallivant without much ado, and my grandad Noel, who always recognises my walk no matter how long I've been gone.

To Billy Cantwell of the *Irish Echo* for giving me the opportunity to stay in Sydney and whose help and advice were invaluable in finishing this book, and to John Roper, who lent me his ear when it was most needed. Also to Joe, Sue and Shane at the *Irish Echo*.

To my friend Ronnie Bellew for all his advice at an early stage and who helped mould this project into what it has become. To my mentor Declan O'Brien, who taught me everything I know about journalism. To Ken Whelan and Mick Cunningham, whose friendship and wisdom has proven invaluable over the years and to Liam Hayes and everyone else at Gazette Group Newspapers in Lucan, who gave me my first start.

To Ger Power, Joey Byrne, Joey Cassidy, Tommy Somers and Mark Moran, who kept me company along the way, and to Darragh Brennan, Cro Dooley, Cian Fleming and all the Mayo girls who gave us a 2007 Christmas and New Year to remember in Sydney.

To Kevin Roche and Róisín Hayden and fellow Saturday Club founders JJ Haren and Brian O'Keeffe of Ballygunner fame, Brian's better half Mairéad Hanrick, the world's proudest Piltown man Eddie Butler, the incomparable Mick Fogarty, the human hurling encyclopaedia Stevie Lonnergan and to the Nissans and Ronan at Durty Nelly's, who tolerated us every Saturday afternoon throughout the season and beyond.

To Brian Larkin and Mick Dowling for looking after the shop at home while I'm away. To Ciarán Phillips, Johnny Cronin, Peter Chambers and Stephen Doran, who have kept me constantly entertained on email from the other side of the world.

To everyone at Lucan Sarsfields GAA club, who fostered my love for the GAA. In particular to my late friend Billy Gogarty, Tommy Clyne, Tony Clarke, Jim Quinn, Pat Glover, Mick Power, Kevin Brennan, Vincent O'Connor, Seán Ó Lanagáin, Eoin and Siobhan Mullarkey and to everyone else at the club who looked after me so well over the years.

To Fergal McCauley from PJ O'Brien's in Sydney, Liam Briggs, Neil Adamson, Lar Collins, Damien Silke, Mark French and Mark Collins and everyone else in Sydney's best bar, The Welcome Hotel, and to Peter Boylan, who joins me regularly in making sure they remain in profit.

To Lorna Markey, Marty Hennessy, Ronan Cassidy, Phil McLoughlin, future Taoiseach Louise Kelly, Danielle Ryan, Lisa Carson and Hugh O'Reilly in Sydney and Rebecca Kiernan and Aisling Conway in Ireland.

To the Lucan girls, Sheena, Maria, Louise, Fiona, Trish, Elaine and Linda, who looked after me in Bondi when I landed first, and to Niamh and Nicola, who arrived from Melbourne later on, and to Leah and Marie back in Lucan.

To Daithí Hanley and Donal McCarthy in Dubai, Mikey Fahy in Dalian, Colin Saunders in Beijing, Louise Weste, Joe Power, Emer Carty, Josh Bizmanovsky and everyone in China's greatest city, Shenzhen.

To Fergal Power in Hong Kong, Sean Hoy in Hanoi and Steve Kinlough in Saigon, to John Campbell in Bangkok and Eoin Duggan in Kuala Lumpur. To Peter Ryan and Paraic McGrath in Singapore, who were unbelievably supportive and helpful in this project from the very beginning.

To future GAA President Brian Deane, Eamonn Eastwood and Liam O'Hara from McAnallen's, Mark Tobin, Declan Maher, Paddy Phelan and all the lads from the Shamrocks, and to everyone from the NSW GAA.

To Liam O'Keeffe, Mick O'Malley, Sean Cullen (you saved my life that day!), Kevin McGarry, Colin Fitzsimons and Silvi Johnson in Auckland, Liam Reidy and John O'Flynn from the San Fran GAA and Conor and Ronan O'Neill for their tour of San Francisco by night.

To Billy Lawless, Kieren Aherne, Kieren Fahy and Trevor and Mick O'Donoghue in Chicago, and to Eugene Kyne from the New York GAA. To Dave Hutton in Clarke's and Tyrone Mickey from Bar 43 in Sunnyside.

Also to Paul and Lori Dalton, Ray and Stephanie Butler, Gemma and Dave Higgins and everyone else from the extended Dalton family who looked after me so well in my time in Boston. Also to Gay and Theresa and the Larkin and Cronin families.

To my editor Deborah Warner, with grateful thanks for all your patience, and everyone else at Mainstream. To everyone else I've left out, you know who you are, thank you very much.

And finally to the Dublin senior teams, who never let it get boring for us tortured fans by always leaving room for improvement. Na Sairsealaigh, Na Ceiltigh is Na Shamróigi Abú!

Go raigh míle maith agat gach duine.

JoRo